Cares melt away… when you kneel in your garden.

Author unknown

Quilts in Red and Green

and the Women Who Made Them

by Nancy Hornback and Terry Clothier Thompson

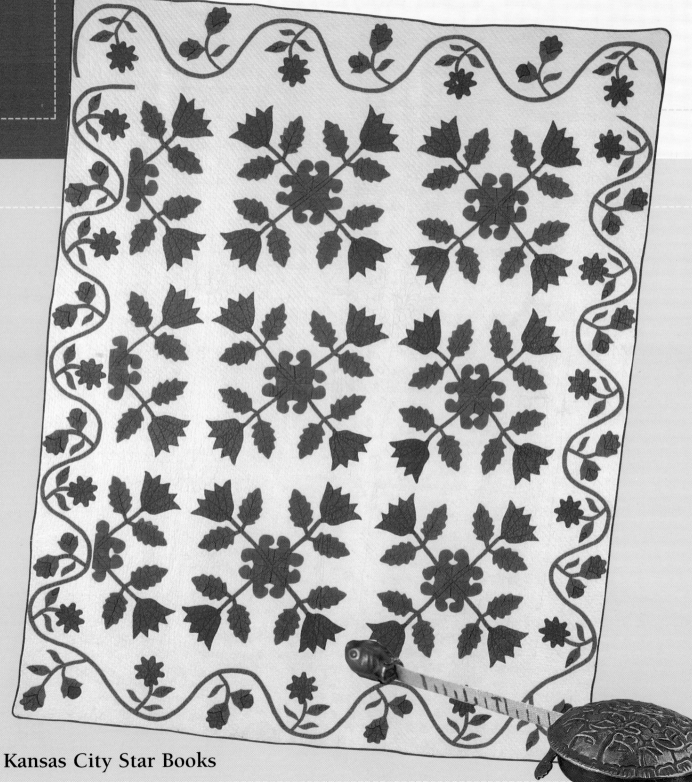

Kansas City Star Books

Quilts in Red and Green
and the Women Who Made Them

by Nancy Hornback and Terry Clothier Thompson

Editor: Judy Pearlstein
Design: Cheryl Johnson, S&Co. Design
Photography: Aaron Leimkuehler
Production Assistance: Jo Ann Groves

Published by Kansas City Star Books
1729 Grand, Kansas City, Missouri 64108
All rights reserved
Copyright © 2006 by The Kansas City Star Co.

First edition, first printing
ISBN 10: 1-933466-11-1
ISBN 13: 978-1-933466-11-8

Printed in the United States of America
by Walsworth Publishing Co.

To order copies, call StarInfo (816-234-4636)

www.PickleDish.com

Thank you to the lenders of quilts:
Gerry Craig and Nelson Smith
Lois Coberly
Jacqualine Byers Frisbie
Sarah Godbey
Georgia Hindman
Paula G. McFarland
Neva Jane Upp
Wichita-Sedgwick County Historical Museum
Ollideen S. Wright

Special thanks to:
Barb Fife for making the batik blocks
Gail Hand for drafting the quilting patterns

Antique sewing tools:
Gail Hand
Mary N. Williams

Others who helped:
Catherine Byers
Leon Cuppet
Mary Beth Craig-Oatley
Jamie Frazier-Tracy
Warren Forsythe
Pamela D. Kingsbury
Bonnie McCampbell Flynn
David McCampbell
Robert A. Puckett
Kate Rowden
Mindy Sorenson
Carol Woodworth

Photographs of some of the quilts, originally taken in
1992 for the *Quilts in Red and Green* exhibit at the
Wichita-Sedgwick County Historical Museum:
Jim Meyer

PickleDish.com
The Quilter's Home Page

KANSAS CITY STAR QUILTS

Table of Contents

1

Nancy Hornback

Nancy Hornback is a fourth-generation Californian, descendant of Missourians who migrated west on the Overland Trail in the 1840s. In 1967, Nancy reversed the direction and moved with her family back to the Midwest. Her interest in quilts began after she inherited a mid-1800s applewood and maple, low-post, cannon-ball rope bed and had acquired two more antique beds. She decided that quilts would be appropriate coverings for the beds and set out to make some. Since she had grown up on the desert and had never seen a quilt being made, and didn't know anyone else who was quilting, she taught herself to quilt from library books. Before long she knew her favorite part of quilting was appliqué.

Nancy was a board member of the Kansas Quilt Project and served as its quilt discovery day coordinator. She wrote a chapter on "19th Century Red and Green Appliqué Quilts" for *Kansas Quilts and Quilters*, published in 1993 by the University Press of Kansas. Nancy researches, lectures, curates quilt shows, and makes quilts. She lives in Wichita, Kansas with her husband Terry. They raised five sons and two daughters and now have eighteen grandchildren.

Terry Clothier Thompson

Terry Clothier Thompson makes her home in Lawrence, Kansas and works in her new studio located in her backyard. There she teaches classes on quilt dating to small groups of women who want to know about the old fabric in quilts, and their history. FabriCamp is taught on Friday, Saturday, and Sunday during the late spring, summer and early fall.

Terry also designs and writes books for Peace Creek Patterns, owned and operated by Terry's daughter Shannon and her husband Kent Richards. These books are about Terry's pioneering family and the quilts of the 1800-1940's period of America's history. Terry designs marking tools for appliquers. The Vine Line, and the new Borderline tools may be found in quilt shops or ordered from the web site.

Terry also has written two books for *The Kansas City Star, Four Block Quilts*, and her most recent book, *Libertyville*.

For fun, Terry grows flowers to press, then designs small still life pictures using old fabrics, lace, and crocheted work. Two children, four grandchildren, and a fifteen-year-old stitch group that meets every week, keep her out of trouble most of the time.

Read Terry's newsletter at terrythompson.com to see what she's doing in her studio. Her e-mail address is terrythompson@sunflower.com.

Terry Thompson and Nancy Hornback first met in 1986 in New York City during the Great American Quilt Festival. Sitting next to each other in the lobby of the Roosevelt Hotel, Nancy introduced herself and they began talking about the Kansas Quilt Project. Through documenting quilts during 1986 and 1987, they became friends. Both were so captivated by the red and green appliqué quilts they were seeing at discovery days, they vowed they would someday work together on a red and green appliqué venture.

In 1992 Nancy wrote a catalog and curated an exhibit of red and green appliqué quilts at the Wichita-Sedgwick County Historical Museum as a thesis project for a master's degree. Terry took the path of designing patterns, teaching, and lecturing about the history of 19th century appliqué. Now they have decided it is time to act on their 20-year old desire to share their enthusiasm for these beautiful quilts.

The ten appliqué patterns in this book are being published for the first time. They reflect a creative energy and uniqueness of design not often seen. This played a large part in our selections. It amazes us to think that after more than 150 years, red and green appliqué quilts still excite the eye and inspire us to recreate their beauty.

We were fascinated by the sophisticated quilting that surrounded the appliqué designs. We realized these stunning 19th century quilting patterns could also be sewn by today's skilled traditional hand quilters as well as by our talented machine quilters.

With one exception, these quilts were made in the comforts of the women's established homes before they migrated to the Great Plains. In learning about these ordinary, yet extraordinary women, we have come to admire the strength, bravery and resourcefulness they revealed as they settled the frontier.

Women who came to the Great Plains from eastern states during the last half of the 19th century brought with them utilitarian objects for their new homes, including quilts. Quilts functioned not only as useful, but also decorative items of bedding. One type particularly worthy of attention for its decorative features is the appliquéd quilt that displayed bold, exuberant floral patterns in bright colors of red and green. The ten quilts in this book are examples of this distinctive quilt type, chosen from a study of 147 such quilts registered in 1987-88 by the Kansas Quilt Project. Made between 1840 and 1895, these quilts are evidence of a migration path that stretched from Pennsylvania through the Ohio Valley states to the Midwest.

Most of the quilts appliquéd in the nineteenth century used a predominantly red and green color scheme against a white background. Red and green fabrics were readily available by 1840, making it possible for quilt makers to carry out what was already a popular color scheme. These colors were used in homes during the first half of the 1800s for drapes, walls, carpets, and table covers. The combination of red and green was prevalent in floral designs in American decorative arts in the period just before the quilts were made. Appliqué quilt patterns were usually floral. Many displayed elaborate quilting and fine workmanship. The white backgrounds of the red and green quilts provided generous space for expert stitching to be prominently displayed. By mid-19th century, quilt makers were still extremely proficient in needle skills. The vogue for red and green appliqué quilts began about 1840, peaked at mid-century, and declined after the Civil War.

Red and green appliqué quilts first appeared during a general upsurge in American quilt making. What had been a popular art form among well-to-do women spread to a growing middle class and was flourishing. Textile factories were producing affordable cotton fabrics. Social changes made needlework an acceptable, even ideal activity for women. European immigrants to the mid-Atlantic region brought with them, not the skills of quilt making, but a love for bright colors and decoration that may have figured into the creation of the red and green appliqué quilts. The atmosphere in early 19th century America was one of restlessness and optimism: there was a willingness to try new things. Migration to the frontier West was important in the spread of ideas, including those that influenced the development of quilt making.

Until this time, the favored method of appliqué was one in which realistic motifs—for example, flowers, birds and trees—were cut from printed chintz fabrics and sewed to a background cloth. By 1840, however, a woman could buy the less costly cottons, either solid-colored or small-scale printed calicoes. No longer restricted to cutting figures from expensive chintzes, she was now free to choose her own appliqué subject matter, and to determine the shapes of the cut-outs for

herself. This shift in technique was basic to the beginnings of the red and green quilts. It gave the quilt maker an opportunity to experiment and invent, while at the same time it created a need for appliqué patterns.

From the known family histories that came with the Kansas red and green appliqué quilts, backgrounds of the quilts' makers were determined. Ethnically, they were German, English, Scotch-Irish, Irish and Welsh. Most of the quilts were made in points of migration, the greater numbers being from Ohio, Indiana, Illinois, and Pennsylvania. Ninety-five percent of the quilt makers recorded religious affiliations as Protestant, with five percent Catholic. Almost all lived in either rural areas or small towns. Middle-class backgrounds are suggested by the occupations of the husbands, for example farmers, dry goods merchants, and cabinetmakers. Overall, we conclude that the quilts makers were rural, middle-class women.

General Directions
Coxcomb and Currant pattern as an example

Use these practical directions from Terry Clothier Thompson to guide you in making your quilt.

Read through all directions before beginning

- Prewash all fabrics.
- We are using a coxcomb pattern as an example. Add 1/4" seam allowance as you cut out the appliqués.
  To begin, prepare the background block by cutting a 20 1/2" square. Remember, fabric is 40-45" wide so you will get 2 blocks per cut.
- Fold square in half, then in half again.
- Press on folded lines. Then fold square on the diagonal and press diagonal lines. These folded/pressed lines serve as a placement guide for the appliqués.

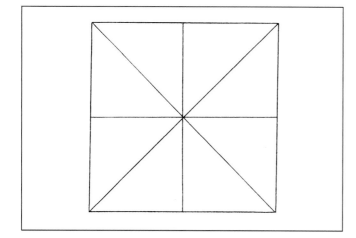

- To prepare appliqués, cut a template of each appliqué. You may stack your fabric and cut several layers at once, but you will need to draw around the template on each piece to give you a pencil "turn under" line.
- Draw around templates on the right side of the fabric. Cut out 1/4" from pencil line as no seam allowance has been added to the patterns. Cut one color at a time.

- Historically all appliqués are laid out on the background block, pinned and basted in place, using the pressed lines as a guide. Before this step is taken, however, appliqué the flower or center rosette units together before placing them on a block. It is much easier to sew smaller units together separately than on the block.

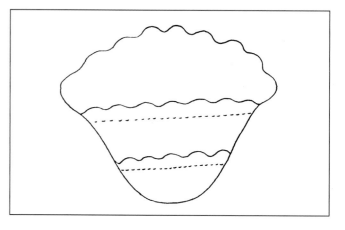

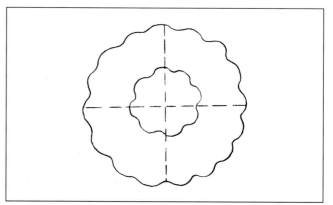

- Now lay out all prepared appliqués, following the pressed lines as a guide. Beginning in the center, pin and baste 1/2" from the raw edge, remove pins and appliqué in place, tucking the ends of stems and leaves a good 1/4" – 1/2" under so raw edges do not appear as you sew.

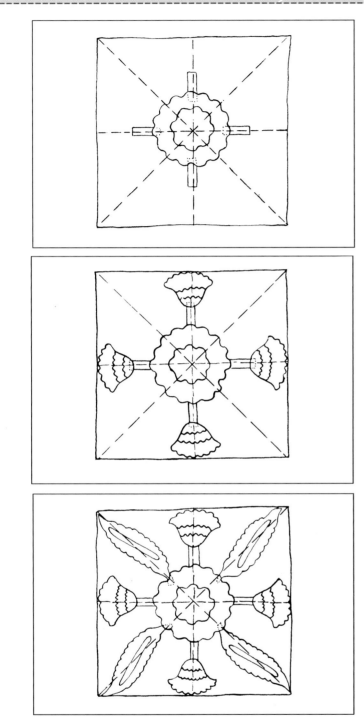

the pencil line 1/4" and basted. This prepares the edges ahead of appliquéing. Yes, it is an extra step, but the beginner has greater success and will love to appliqué. Of course as one improves this step may be eliminated; however, I still pre-baste if several units are to be layered.

- Intermediate and advanced appliquérs may use the blind stitch or machine appliqué using freezer paper techniques. Consult your local quilt shop or quilt guild for appliqué classes, learn all the techniques, then choose what is best for you. In taking a class, you will learn so much more about appliqué techniques, and you will be supporting your shop or guild at the same time. Do not cut out behind appliqués, as the appliqués need the support of the background block. (You will have to cut backs out when using the freezer paper technique to remove the paper.) Set finished blocks on square or on point.

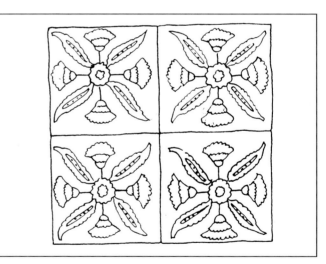

- Now the sewing part. I strongly suggest that beginners appliqué in the top running stitch, even pre-basting the appliqués before pinning and basting to the block. This just means that all raw edges of the appliqués are turned under on

Borders: I do not miter borders. I sew the top and bottom first, then the sides.

• Find the center of the border and swag. Center swag at center of border, then everything is laid out from the center.

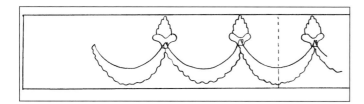

• Appliqué borders separately from blocks, then sew to body of quilt placing corner swags to meet the two connecting borders.
• Remove all basting.

To quilt, use background filler patterns for the empty spaces between blocks, such as clamshell, double lines, feathers, or diamonds. Any design will look terrific on these quilts.

Marking Your Quilt:
• Trace the quilt patterns on to your quilt top by placing the top over the printed pattern, then lightly draw with a #2 pencil over the lines or make small dots. If the pattern lines are too light to show through the quilt fabric, darken the patterns with a black marker. Tops may also be marked from the top with commercial plastic templates. Straight lines and grids may be marked with a yardstick. Use a #2 lead pencil. It will usually fade away as you quilt or with the first or second washing, if lines are not too dark. If your fabric is dark, you can create a light table by using a storm window propped between two chairs with a lamp underneath to illuminate the design. Trace, using a white lead dressmaker's pencil or art pencil.

Quilting:
Place backing (wrong side up), batting, the quilt top (right side up), on a flat surface. Pin and baste all three layers together, smoothing wrinkles. Arrange quilt in hoop. Start in center, working toward the edge, using a single thread and knot, bringing needle through all three layers from underneath side of quilt. Pop the knot through the back layer, thereby securing the knot in the batting layer. Now you are ready to quilt. With the needle at a 45-degree angle, take small running stitches, catching all three layers. To finish off, run the needle under the top layer of the quilt the length of the needle, then trim off the extra thread. (For more information about appliqué, refer to Terry's book, *Four Block Quilts* from *The Kansas City Star* at your quilt shop.)

- Bind edges. (I like to make a bias binding.) Attach a sleeve. Sign and date your quilt, and you are finished.
- To cut out 9 - 20 1/2" background squares, leave yardage folded to cut **20 1/2" squares 2 square blocks at a time.** This includes the seam allowance. Cut borders on the cross grain and piece end to end.

Coxcomb & Currant directions as an example

- Follow General Directions above for preparation of background block and appliqué pieces.
- Appliqué small rosette A to large center flower B. Appliqué calyx C to middle coxcomb D to top coxcomb E.
- Match center of large rosette A-B to center of background block. Pin in place.
- Pin stem F on horizontal and vertical lines. Pin coxcomb units on horizontal and vertical lines, covering the raw edge of stem.
- To reverse appliqué centers of ferns, cut a slit down the center of each fern on the dotted line shown on the pattern piece. Cut fabric for the insert approximately 3" x 11 1/2". (The shape has been outlined on the pattern piece.) DO NOT skimp on this insert piece as you want all raw edges of the slash to disappear onto the insert, and not come up short. Sew insert before basting to block. Appliqué berries H to insert. You may have the background show instead of adding an insert as shown in the quilt.
- Pin ferns G on the diagonal lines, referring to the photo for placement.
- Baste all pieces in place.
- Remove pins and appliqué.
- Sew the blocks together.
- Quilt and bind.

Good Advice
Appliqué techniques
I. Top running stitch appliqué
- Many antique quilts were sewn with a running stitch to secure the appliqué. This basic hand-sewing stitch, the one we use for quilting and piecing, is the easiest hand appliqué stitch. I recommend this technique for beginning appliqué artists because the stitches can be easily seen on the top of the appliqué. The stitch is speedy and you may take three to four stitches at a time. Although this technique flattens the appliqué somewhat, it is secure and gives a finished look. A different colored thread can add a little color or a strong outline to your appliqué.
- Prepare the appliqué by placing the pattern on the top side of the fabric. Trace around the appliqué with a #2 lead pencil. If the fabric is dark, use a chalk pencil. This line is the guideline for turning under the 1/4" seam allowance.
- Cut, adding 1/4" seam allowance around the pencil line.
- I recommend that beginners pre-baste each appliqué piece by turning under the 1/4" seam on the pencil line and basting the edges over. Baste all appliqué patches to the background, tucking under points and raw edges.
- Stitch, gathering your fabric up on your needle as you go, about 1/16 – 1/8" from the edge of the appliquéd piece. You don't want to do a stab stitch (one stitch at a time).
- Use contrasting thread to show your even stitches.

II. Blind stitch
- Pin and baste each layer of the design in place. Knot a thread and bring your needle from the wrong side of the background block and through

the folded edge of the appliqué. Take needle back down thru block and back up again about 1/16" from the last stitch into the fold of the appliqué. Use your needle to turn under the raw edge, press with your finger and hold in place with your thumb. I move my thumb and finger press about 1" ahead of my last stitch. (Finger press 1/2" ahead of the last stitch, using needle to turn under raw edge of appliqué.) This technique gives a rounded "lifted" edge to the appliqué.

Making berries and currants

To make berries and currants (or any round shape), use sticky removable labels found at office supply stores for large, medium and small circles. Place sticky labels on fabric, cut 1/4" seam allowance and glue or hand baste the edges under. Remove labels and appliqué.

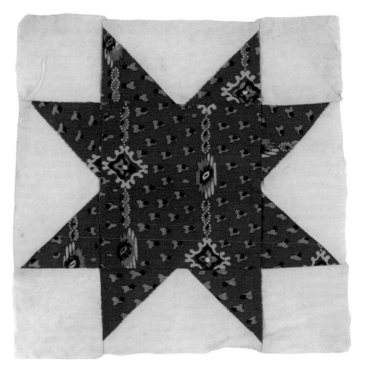

Colors and Fabric

The traditional colors of red, green, pink, chrome yellow and orange, better known as cheddar, appear in the 19ᵗʰ century appliquéd quilts. Because of their special status, women saved them for special occasions, thus sparing the quilts from hard use and harsh laundry methods. However, after 150 years, some quilts show wear and the reds in particular turn a nice shade of pink. The early Turkey red calico could be a blue red or a tomato red shade. In Pennsylvania, quilters substituted a cinnamon red calico for the brighter Turkey reds of the period.

If you prefer a historical look for your antique bedroom furniture, choose the traditional red. If you want a quilt that fits into your more conventional decorating style, choose a nice combination of pinks and a variety of light greens. Barb Fife chose black as a background for her shaded batik fabrics.

As for greens, you may choose the traditional bright, spring greens that look like the early greens or tone down the shades that look good with the pink calicos. Use these greens with the cinnamon reds and pinks for the Pennsylvania German madder in your quilts. Many women used a lovely teal blue in place of green. Blue was not often used, but was not all that uncommon.

Use pink and yellow and cheddar as accent colors, for buds, rosettes, vases, and berries. Background blocks were a light muslin or white, sometimes a shirting. A small print looks nice also. It's very sweet for a girl's bedroom.

Estimated yardage for a 9 block sampler quilt with borders:
For the sampler quilt blocks, choose a nice variety of reds, greens, and accent colors of pink, cheddar, yellow, and gold.
I prefer to mix different shades of the main colors for a less formal quilt.
I suggest you buy:
1/2 to 3/4 yards of 3 or 4 different shades of red and green for a real scrappy look, which is more contemporary. If you prefer to use 1 fabric for each of the red and green, buy at least 2 1/2 to 3 yards of red, and 3 yards of green for bias stems, leaves and border vines. Buy 1 1/2 yards of your accent colors of pink, yellow, cheddar, or gold.
For a 9 - 20" block quilt with 10 1/2" borders, buy 7 1/4 yards. Cut borders on the cross grain.
For 2 1/2" wide finished sashing, buy 2 yards.
Backing fabric for an 86" x 105" quilt with 9 1/2" borders takes 7 1/4 yards.

The average size of each vintage quilt is 85" x 90", so I estimated the yardage for the backgrounds of blocks, borders, appliqués and backings/bindings. These are traditional colors. Choose your favorite colors for your home.

Sarah Pollock's *Rose and Thistle*

Rose and Thistle
Sarah Ann Forsythe Pollock (1829–1912)
Made in Ohio. 81" x 82"
Collection of Paula G. McFarland

Sarah Ann Forsythe was born in 1829 in Guernsey County, Ohio, one of twelve children of Robert and Salley Frame Forsythe. According to her descendants, Sarah made this remarkable quilt when she was between 18 and 20 years old. About 1860, she married Hamilton Pollock. In the early 1870s the Pollock family, which by now included three children, William, Robert and Sarah, moved to Sterling, Kansas. An infant daughter Jennie was buried in the Sterling cemetery in 1875.

That Sarah was a skilled needle worker is evident by her elegant quilting and elaborate stuffed work. Five classical urns and three flower-filled vases are displayed in white background areas. Other stuffed work is in feather, floral, and berry designs. The background is closely quilted in parallel rows less than one-fourth inch apart, adding further emphasis to the stuffed motifs. In stuffed work, the quilt maker quilts a design, turns the quilt to the back and makes openings by parting threads, then adds extra cotton with a blunt instrument, giving the design a raised effect. According to a family story, Sarah used a rose thorn to push the stuffing through the back of her quilt. When we were preparing the quilt for an exhibit in 1992, we were astonished to find a rose thorn still embedded in the quilt's lining, after more than 140 years.

Sarah Ann Forsythe Pollock

The primary motif in Sarah Pollock's quilt is a large geometric flower built up in layers appliquéd in concentric rings, each layer in eight equal divisions. From a red center, the encircling layers are alternately white and red, ending with eight outer lobes of green. Each rosette is surrounded by eight spiky leaves that look like they might belong to thistles. Four small rose wreaths fill the spaces between the flowers.

Rose and Thistle
20" Finished Sampler Block
Stitched by Barb Fife

For 1-20" sampler block

Pattern Pieces

A – Largest rosette, cut 1 green
B – Large rosette, cut 1 red
C – Medium rosette, cut 1 ecru
D – Small rosette, cut 1 red
E – Tiny rosette, cut 1 ecru
F – Rose wreath rosettes, cut 4 red
G – Large leaves, cut 8 green
H – Calyx for bud in wreath, cut 4 green
I – Bud in wreath, cut 4 red
J – Wreath leaf, cut 4 green
K – Wreath circle, cut 1 green 9" diameter
Cut 1 ecru square 20 1/2" for background block.

Sewing

* Follow general directions for block and appliqué units preparation on page 6.
* Begin with rosette A and B. Place B over A with B "hills" matching with A "valleys." Sew C, D, E, to the rosette underneath it, matching hills and valleys.
* Lay appliquéd rosette in center of square. Pin and baste in place. Appliqué large layered rosette.
* Place G leaves at an angle to fit in the 20" square. Pin and baste. You may shorten the length of the stems if you want the leaves straight.
* Appliqué leaves.

For a large 9-block quilt 81" x 81"

Cutting and Assembling

* For Sarah's large quilt, cut 9 – 27 1/2" background squares. This is a different size from the 20" sampler block. Sarah's quilt has no borders, but you certainly may add a chintz or calico border to get the size you need for your bed.
* There are four appliquéd wreaths that fit over the corner seams of the set blocks. Because the squares are larger, the leaves will have more room to go straight out from the rosette. Follow directions for appliqué on page 6.
* Set 9 blocks in 3 rows of 3 blocks. Refer to picture for layout.

Quilting

Background quilting is in 1/4" parallel lines, traveling right over the appliqués. Clusters of grapes, flowers and classical urns and pineapples add to the beauty of the quilt.

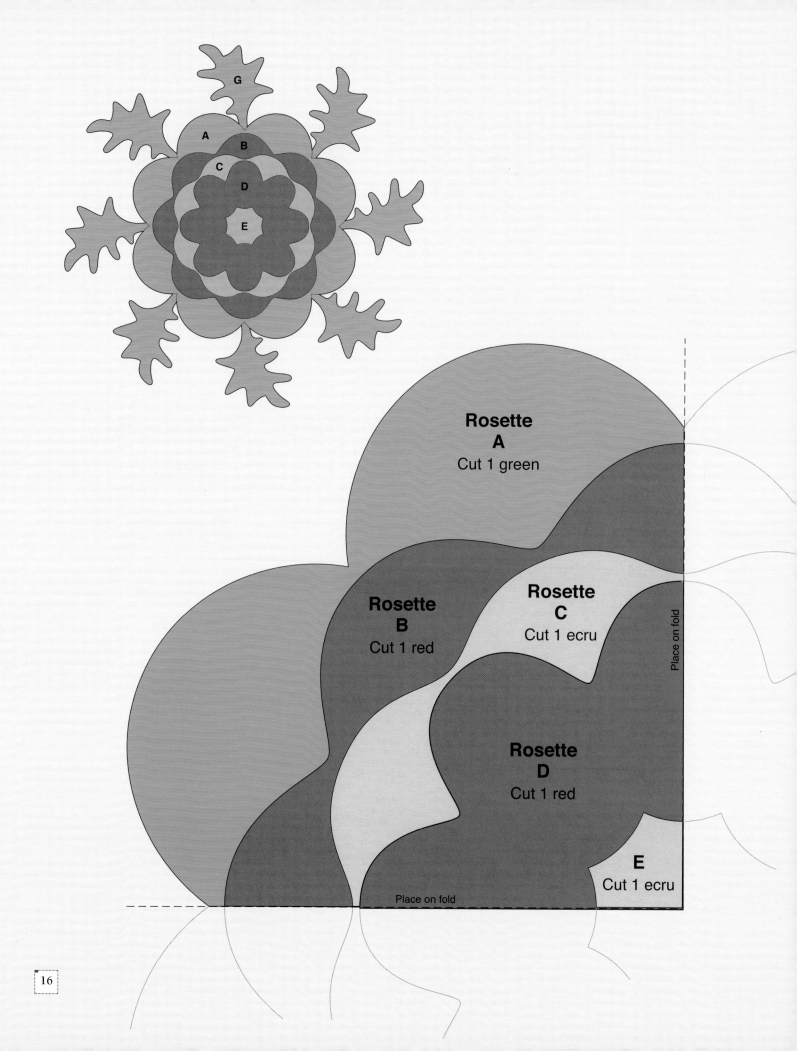

Rosette
A
Cut 1 green

Rosette
B
Cut 1 red

Rosette
C
Cut 1 ecru

Rosette
D
Cut 1 red

E
Cut 1 ecru

Place on fold

Place on fold

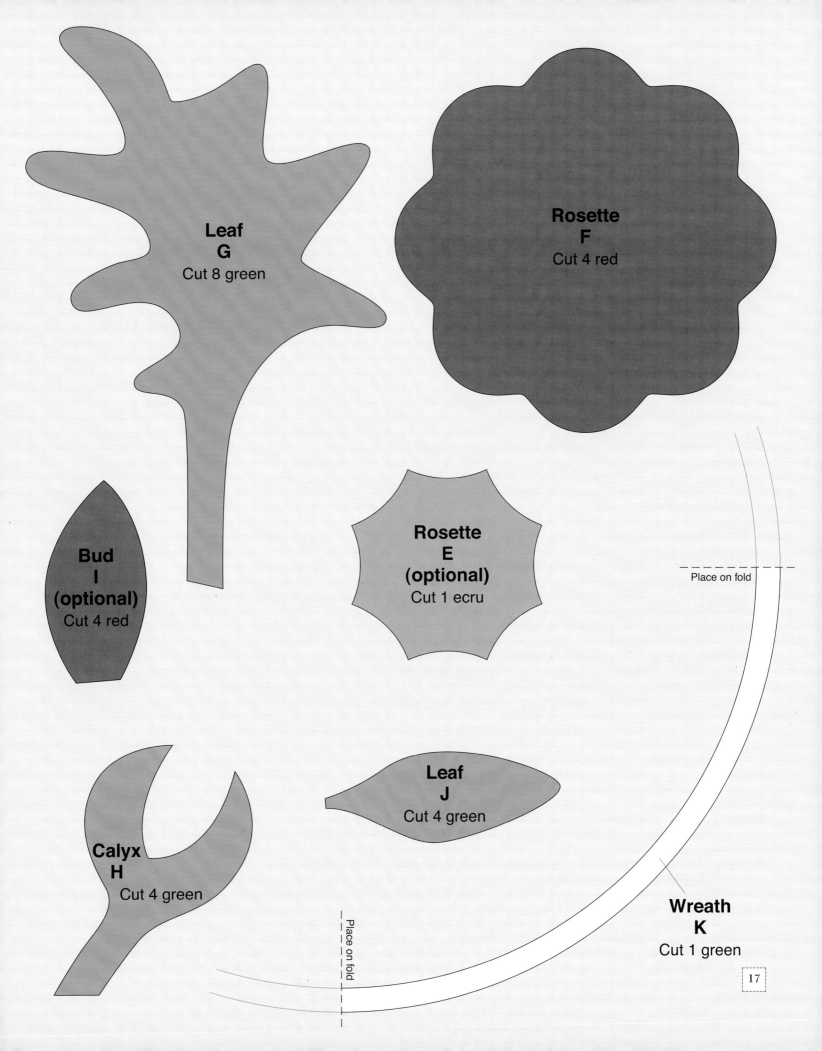

**Leaf
G**

Cut 8 green

**Rosette
F**

Cut 4 red

**Bud
I
(optional)**

Cut 4 red

**Rosette
E
(optional)**

Cut 1 ecru

Place on fold

**Calyx
H**

Cut 4 green

**Leaf
J**

Cut 4 green

**Wreath
K**

Cut 1 green

Place on fold

Evans Family Quilt, attributed to members of
the Evans family. Made in Ohio.
63" x 82"
Collection of Wichita-Sedgwick County
Historical Museum, given in memory of John
Lillie Evans and the Evans family by his
granddaughter Pamela Denman Kingsbury

It is uncertain whether this pot of flowers quilt was made by Pennsylvania-born Maria Evans (1816-1877) or by one of her daughters, Laura, Hannah or Amanda. Perhaps all of them helped make it. The John Evans family was Quaker and had immigrated to this country from Wales. The family's travels in the United States can be traced from inscriptions in books. Maria's husband was, among other things, a teacher and a great reader, purchasing leather-bound literature and history books that have come down in the family. From Philadelphia, John and Maria traveled to Wheeling, West Virginia, later moving across the Ohio River to Wheeling Creek, Ohio. By 1834 John Evans owned a carding mill (see photo). Later the family lived in Daviess County, Indiana. Besides the three daughters, John and Maria Evans raised a son, Lorenzo Dow Evans. Lorenzo's son, John Lillie Evans, left Indiana for St. Louis, where he graduated from medical school. In 1906 he came further west to Wichita to be a physician for the Missouri Pacific Railroad. When John left his Indiana home he brought with him a woven coverlet, a Seth Thomas clock, and the Evans family "Quaker" quilt.

The vase and flowers design on the Evans quilt has been appliquéd in twelve blocks, set on the diagonal. A red vase holds a center stem with a double tulip in red and orange. On the two side stems are red carnations. Quilting is in straight lines, through the appliquéd vase and the flowers. Feathered wreaths with grid centers fill the white spaces. The quilt is bordered on two sides by a meandering vine with stems and buds.

1834 advertisement of John Evans' wool carding mill. Courtesy of Pamela Denman Kingsbury.

Evans Family Quilt Sampler Block
20" Finished
Stitched by Barb Fife

For 1-20" sampler block

Pattern pieces

A – Vase, cut 1 red

B – Bottom petal of lily, cut 1 red (on fold)

C – Center petal of lily, cut 1 red (on fold)

D – Middle petal of lily, cut 1 and cut 1 reverse, gold/cheddar

E – Leaf under lily, cut 1 green and 1 reverse

F – Leaf off vase sides, cut 1 green and 1 reverse

G – Lily bud, cut 2 gold/cheddar

H – Carnation, cut 8 red

I – Carnation center circle, cut 2 cheddar/gold

J – Bud (for border), cut 60 red, 3 per stem

K – Calyx (for border), cut 60 green

L – Carnation stem, cut 1 green and 1 reverse

M – Lily bud stem, cut 2 green

N – Border leaf, cut 6 green

Center stem, cut 1 - 1" x 13 1/2" green

Cut 1 background block 20 1/2"

Sewing

- Prepare all appliqués for hand or machine sewing
- Lay out the vase first on the center crease, then place the center stem, 1" x 13 1/2" in the middle of the vase on the center crease line. Place sewn lily unit at the top of the stem.
- Place the carnation stems in the vase, then the lily buds, stems and leaves as shown in the picture. Pin and baste.
- Pin and baste carnation petals and small center circle over ends of carnation petals.
- Appliqué all units with a blind or running stitch, or by machine. Refer to templates for color and number of pattern pieces.

For large quilt   100 3/4" x 129"

Blocks are set on point.

Cutting

- Cut 12 - 20 1/2" squares for 12 appliquéd background blocks, and 6 - 20 1/2" squares for alternating, quilted blocks.
- For 10 setting triangles, cut 3 - 29 5/8" squares. Cut into 4 triangles (see figure #1) for 10 setting triangles (you will have 2 extra triangles).
- For 4 corner triangles, cut 2 -15 1/8" squares, cut each into 2 triangles (figure #2).
- Cut top and bottom borders 8 1/2" x 101 1/4".
- Cut side borders 8 1/2" x 113 1/2". The quilt has borders on two sides that are appliquéd and two that are only quilted.
- The 8" border vines run right off the edge.

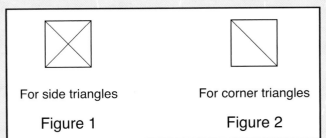

For side triangles   For corner triangles

Figure 1   Figure 2

Setting

- Refer to figures #3 and #4 for setting blocks and borders.

Quilting designs

The appliquéd blocks are quilted in a parallel 1/4" line pattern that fills the background block and goes over the appliquéd pieces. The alternating blocks contain large feather circles, with the same parallel lines filling in the corners. See Quilting section on page 6.

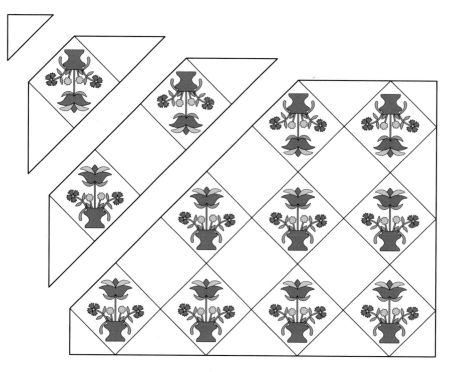

Figure 3

8" x 113"

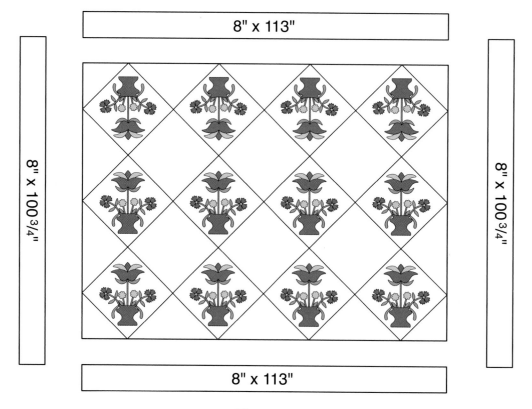

8" x 100 ³/₄"

8" x 100 ³/₄"

8" x 113"

Figure 4

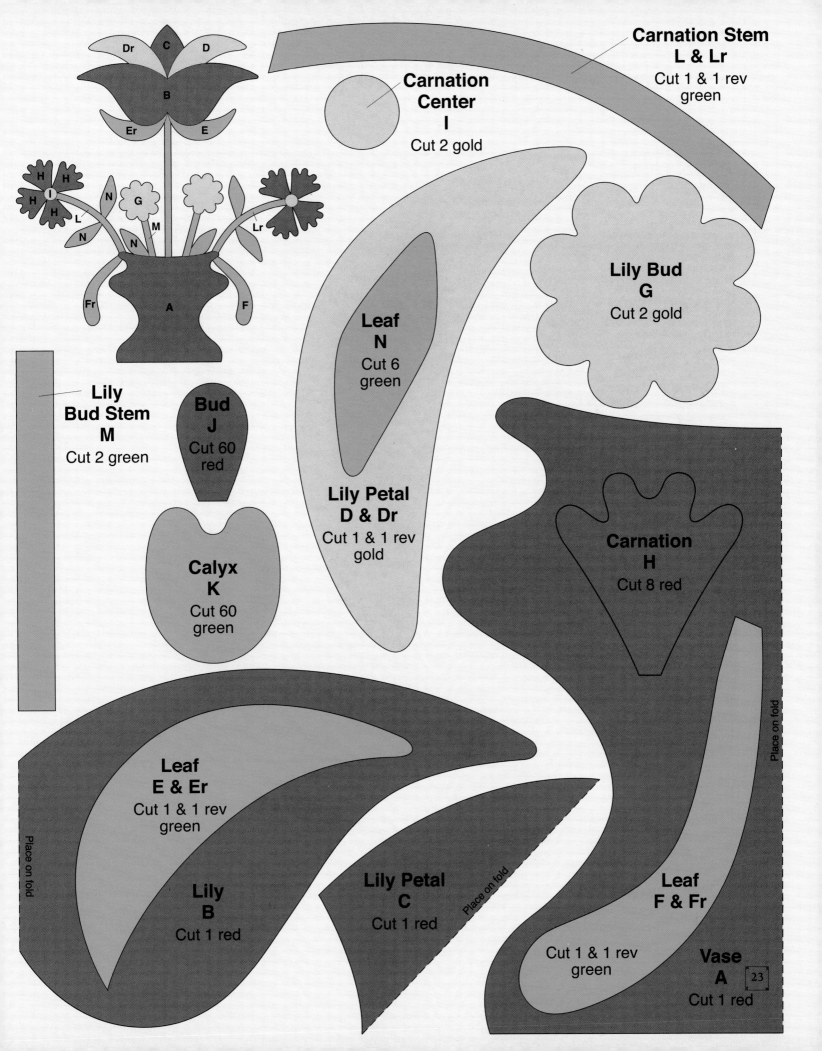

Carnation Stem L & Lr
Cut 1 & 1 rev green

Carnation Center I
Cut 2 gold

Lily Bud G
Cut 2 gold

Leaf N
Cut 6 green

Lily Bud Stem M
Cut 2 green

Bud J
Cut 60 red

Calyx K
Cut 60 green

Lily Petal D & Dr
Cut 1 & 1 rev gold

Carnation H
Cut 8 red

Place on fold

Leaf E & Er
Cut 1 & 1 rev green

Place on fold

Lily B
Cut 1 red

Lily Petal C
Cut 1 red

Place on fold

Leaf F & Fr
Cut 1 & 1 rev green

Vase A
Cut 1 red

23

Rose Tree
Sarah Jane Work Denny (1832-1917)
Made in Pennsylvania. 85" x 93"
Collection of Gerry Craig and Nelson Smith

The 1850 census shows Sarah Jane Work to be the fourth of seven children raised by James and Margaret Work. Sarah was born in 1832 in Buffalo, Pennsylvania. The Works were involved in textiles; they raised sheep and did their own wool carding in both Ireland and Pennsylvania. Descendants believe one of Sarah's sisters helped make the Rose Tree quilt. Perhaps it was her older sister Nancy or her younger sister Isabella.

Sarah married Will Denny in 1857. The marriage took place at 5:00 o'clock in the morning to allow for an early start on a wedding trip to West Virginia. Sarah wore a hand-stitched wedding dress of black satin. Great-great-granddaughter Gerry Craig told us that according to Great Aunt Ona McQuown, besides the Rose Tree, Sarah made another beautiful quilt, a blue and white Jacob's Ladder, and wouldn't marry Will until she finished it. However, another descendant remembers another version, Aunt Ona saying that Sarah would not have a child until she finished the quilt. Will and Sarah Denny brought their family to Kansas by train in 1879 in response to a land development advertisement in their Presbyterian church newspaper. They made their home in Walton, in Harvey County, Kansas.

Four-generation photo, 1916. Seated, Sarah Jane Work Denny holding her great-grandson Harry Earl Molzen; sitting next to her, Sarah's daughter Nettie Denny McQuown; standing, granddaughter Myrtle McQuown Molzen. Courtesy of Mary Beth Craig-Oatley.

Sarah Denny's Rose Tree quilt combines several design elements that are distinctive in 19th century appliqué quilts. The pattern is made up of an urn into which is placed a center sprouting flower stem that holds a pomegranate. The U-shaped symmetrical side stems bear the same pomegranate shapes. The sprouting flower is a rosette. Three rosette motifs, surrounded by leaves, are repeated in a center panel that divides the quilt. Rosettes and pomegranates are seen again in the appliquéd vine border. Sophisticated quilted and stuffed motifs include a pair of classical urns filled with a lavish display of flowers and pineapples, as well as six narrow panels of berry-laden vines. The exceptionally fine background quilting varies between thirteen and nineteen stitches to the inch (counted on the top of the quilt).

Black satin wedding dress made by Sarah Work for her 1857 wedding to Will Denny. Courtesy of Mary Beth Craig-Oatley.

Rose Tree Sampler Block
20" Finished
Stitched by Barb Fife

For 1 - 20" sampler block

Pattern pieces

A – Center star of large rosette, cut 1 gold, yellow, pink or red

(NOTE – in the picture of the original vintage quilt, there is a larger pink rosette. I took that out to make the smaller rosette and stems fit the 20" block.)

B – Center rosette, cut 1 red or pink

C – Large rosebud, cut 3 red

D – Leaves, cut 3 green

E – Center of large bud, cut 3 green

F – Vase, cut 1 green

G – Leaf for alternate block, cut 7 green

H – Block and border leaf, cut 18 green for block and 36 for border.

I – Bud leaf, cut 6 green, 3 gold

J – Rosette stem, cut 1 green

Curved stem, cut a 1" x 36" bias strip.

Cut a 20 1/2" background block.

Sewing

- Layer star A over rosette B for center rosette.
- For buds, lay the green center bud E over red bud C, then leaves D around bud.
- Pin, baste and appliqué all units before placing on background. Refer to picture.
- Center vase at center bottom of block. Fold block in half and press a line for placement of vase F, stem J, rosette and center bud unit.
- Pin and baste all above units on this line, using the finished 1/2" bias strips for the stem coming out of the rosette and for curved vines on each side of the center.
- Place right and left bud units at end of stems. Place large leaves H on stems, and small leaves I over buds.

For large quilt   93" x 93"

I increased the size of the background block from 20" to 21" with 15" borders to accommodate the rosettes, buds and deep, curved vine of the original quilt. Follow the same preparations for the 21 1/2" cut backgrounds and appliqués in the sampler block directions.

Cutting

- Cut 6 - 21 1/2" background blocks for the rose trees, and 3 - 21 1/2" background blocks for the 3 alternate blocks with the rosette and leaf patterns.
- Cut top and bottom borders 15 1/2" x 63 1/2". Cut 2 side borders 15 1/2" x 93 1/2." See diagram on page 45.

Setting

Set 9 finished blocks, 3 blocks in 3 rows using the picture as your guide. The center of the quilt is 63" x 63".

Quilting full quilt

The background quilting is a 1/2" square grid, traveling right over the appliqués. Feathers, pineapples and grape clusters surround the blocks. See the quilting section for quilting the Rose Tree.

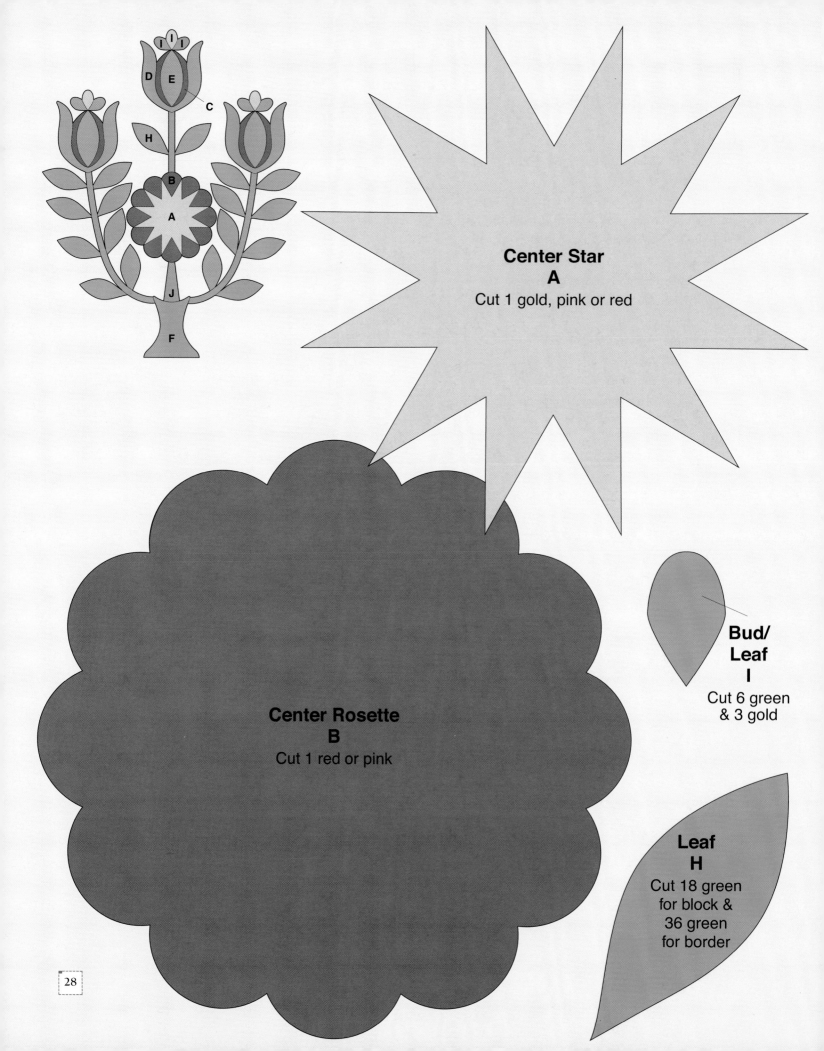

**Center Star
A**
Cut 1 gold, pink or red

**Bud/
Leaf
I**
Cut 6 green
& 3 gold

**Center Rosette
B**
Cut 1 red or pink

**Leaf
H**
Cut 18 green
for block &
36 green
for border

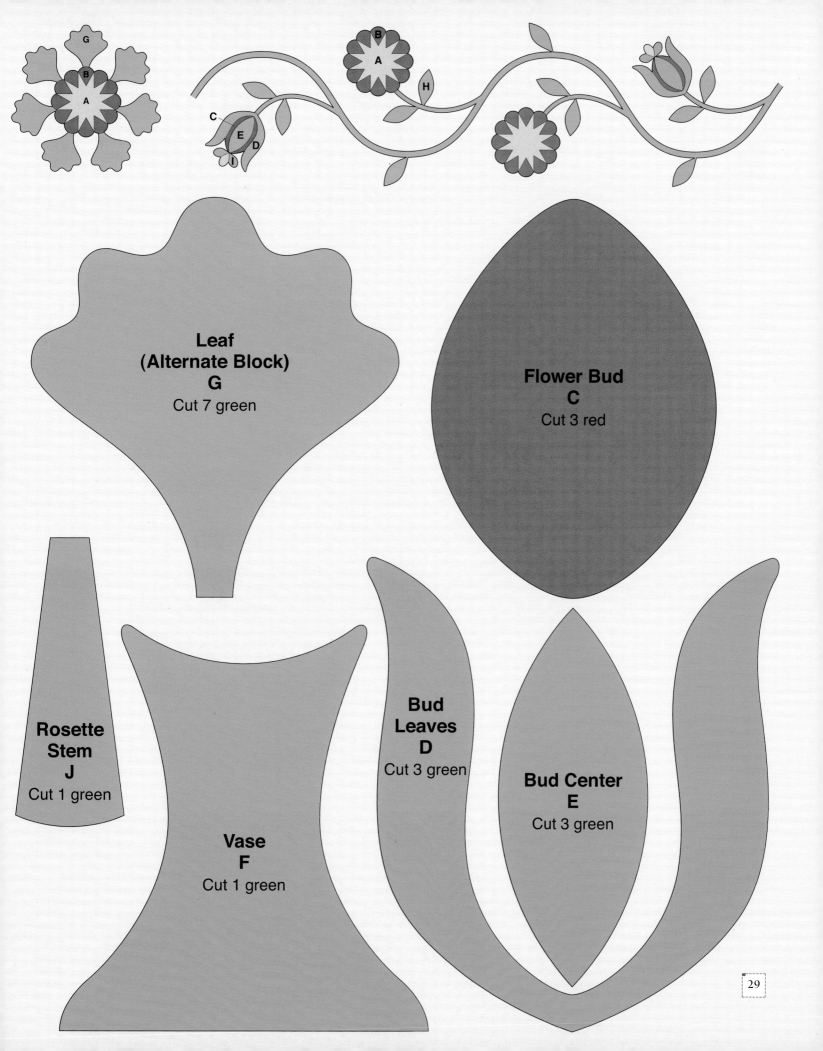

**Leaf
(Alternate Block)
G**

Cut 7 green

**Flower Bud
C**

Cut 3 red

**Rosette
Stem
J**

Cut 1 green

**Bud
Leaves
D**

Cut 3 green

**Bud Center
E**

Cut 3 green

**Vase
F**

Cut 1 green

29

15" x 63"

15" x 93"

15" x 93"

15" x 63"

What a pity flowers can utter no sound!
A singing rose, a whispering violet, a murmuring honeysuckle,...
... Oh what a rare and exquisite miracle would these be!

Henry Ward Beecher

Plumes and Coxcombs
Catherine Johnson Cover (1830-1888)
Made in Pennsylvania. 84" x 84"
Collection of Martha Jo Langhofer

**Patterns for this quilt are not available in
this book but are planned for a future,
companion book to** *Quilts in Red and Green.*

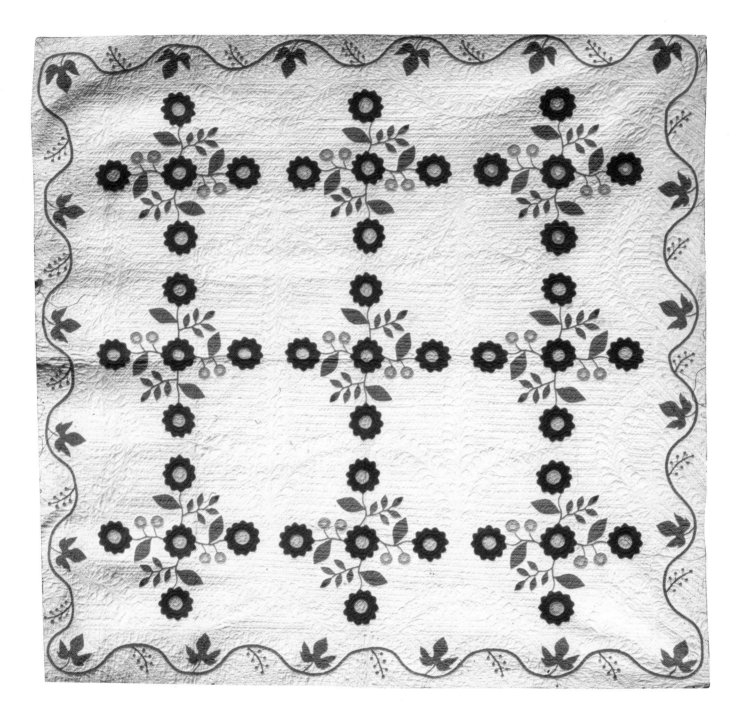

Rose Appliqué
Isabel Andrews Wilson (1812-1883)
Made in Ohio. 77" x 79"
Collection of Lois Coberly

Isabel Andrews Wilson (1812-1883) was the daughter of Mary Cain and Thomas Brown Andrews. She made her Rose Appliqué quilt while living near Amity, Ohio. After the death of her husband, Jonas, she came to Kansas to homestead in western Coffey County. The 1870 federal census for Lyon County shows her at age 56 living in the household of her brother, Andrew Jackson Andrews. Her occupation is listed as seamstress.

Since Isabel had no children, her quilt was inherited by Carvallo Andrews, a nephew who led an adventuresome life. Carvallo ran away from home at the age of eleven to become a cowboy, but his father went to get him at the Oklahoma border. Later he left again, to Texas, and this time he was successful. Later treks took him to Wyoming, West Virginia and Wisconsin. Eventually he returned to Kansas to make a permanent home.

Today the quilt belongs to Lois Coberly, great-great niece of Isabel Wilson and granddaughter of Carvallo Andrews. Lois remembers a story told by her mother, Vella Andrews Gunkel. Vella was living about seven miles southeast of Emporia. It seems that a woman from Emporia wanted to borrow the quilt to copy it. Vella would not let the quilt out of her house, but she allowed the woman to come to her home to copy it. The woman's copied quilt won a first prize at the Kansas State Fair. Could this woman have been one of the famed seven Emporia quiltmakers?[1]

In Isabel's appliquéd rose pattern, the floral forms in the four corners of the block repeat the shape of the center motif. Green leaves, sprigs of pink blossoms and red buds are on the gracefully curved slender stems. Clusters of green grapes on narrow appliquéd red stems are suspended from the undulating grapevine in the border. The diagonal set of the nine appliquéd blocks creates large expanses of white space that are filled by quilted double lines and feather sprays.

[1]Barbara Brackman, "Emporia, 1925-1950: Reflections on a Community." In *Kansas Quilts and Quilters*, Brackman *et al*, (Lawrence, KS: University Press of Kansas, 1993), 107-125.

Carvallo Andrews, nephew of Isabel Andrews Wilson

Woman's wrapper, c. 1875. Background fabric is actual size 19th century fabric, possibly made for a table.

Quiltmaker's tools of the trade

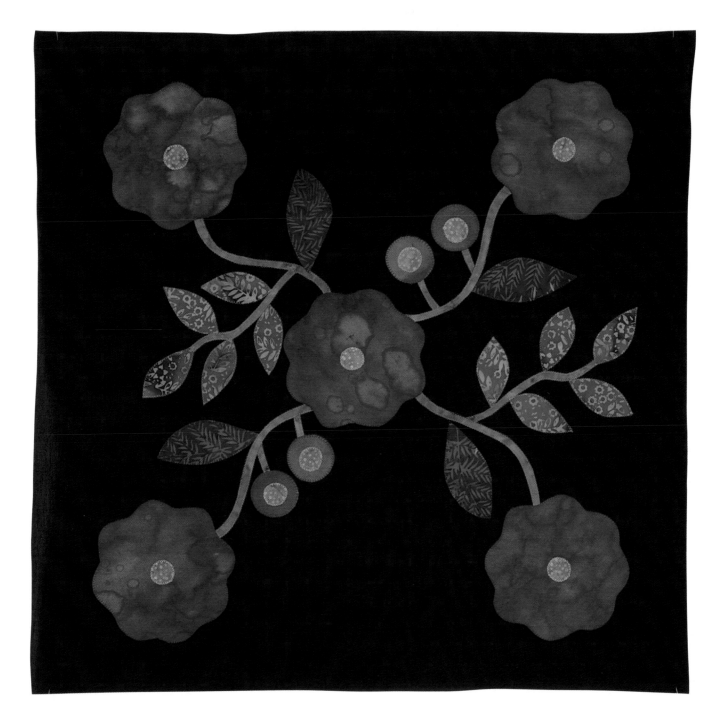

Rose Appliqué
20" Finished
Stitched by Barb Fife

For 1- 20" sampler block

Pattern Pieces

A – Rosette, cut 5 red
B – Rose hips, cut 9 pink
C – Center circle of rose and hips, cut 9 yellow
D – Border berries, cut 140 green
E – Rose bud, cut 2 red
F – Bud calyx, cut 2 green
G – Leaf, cut 8 green
H – Rose leaf, cut 4 green
I – Border leaf, cut 20 green
J – Border leaf stem, cut 20 green
K – Border berry stem, cut 20 red
L – Main rose stem, cut 4 green
M – Rose bud stem, cut 2 green
Cut background block 20 1/2" square.

Sewing

- Prepare appliqués for hand or machine appliqué.
- Place prepared rosettes A in center and on the ends of the four corner stems.
- Refer to the picture and place stems, buds, and leaves, rose hips on block.
- Pin and baste all appliqué in place.
- Appliqué with a running stitch or blind stitch.

For large quilt 98 3/4" x 98 3/4"

- Make nine appliquéd blocks following directions for the sampler block, using the same 20 1/2" squares for a 20" finished block. Set on point.
- Cut 4 - 20 1/2" squares out of the same background for the alternate plain setting blocks.
- For the side triangles, cut 2 - 29 5/8" squares of the background fabric. Cut the 2 squares into four triangles, (see figure #1) for eight setting triangles.
- For corner triangles, cut two squares 15 1/8". Cut on the diagonal for four corner triangles. See figure #2.

For side triangles   For corner triangles

Figure 1   Figure 2

- Set the nine blocks on point following the diagram on page 37 for setting triangles and corners.
- Cut top and bottom borders 7 1/2" x 85 1/4".
- Cut two side borders 7 1/2" x 99 1/4".
- Adjust your borders to fit your bed.
- Appliqué 1/2" bias vine with leaf I, placing stems and berries by referring to photograph.

Quilting

Background is quilted in 2 parallel lines, 1/4" apart, with 1" between lines right over the appliqués. Feathers surround the appliquéd roses. See detail, page 104.

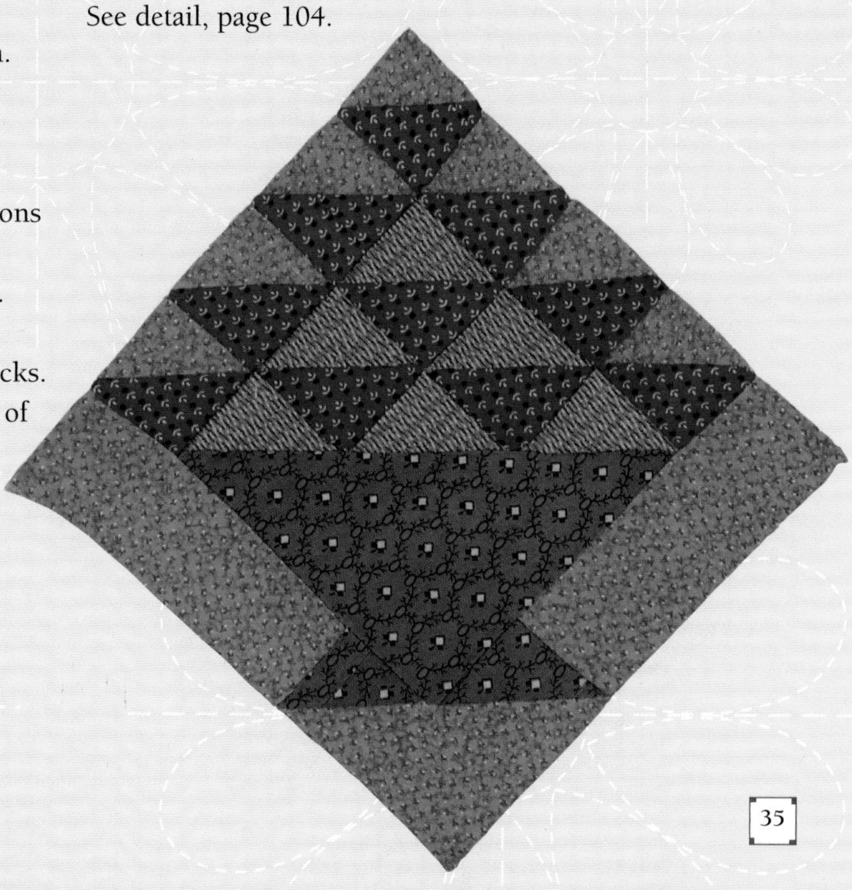

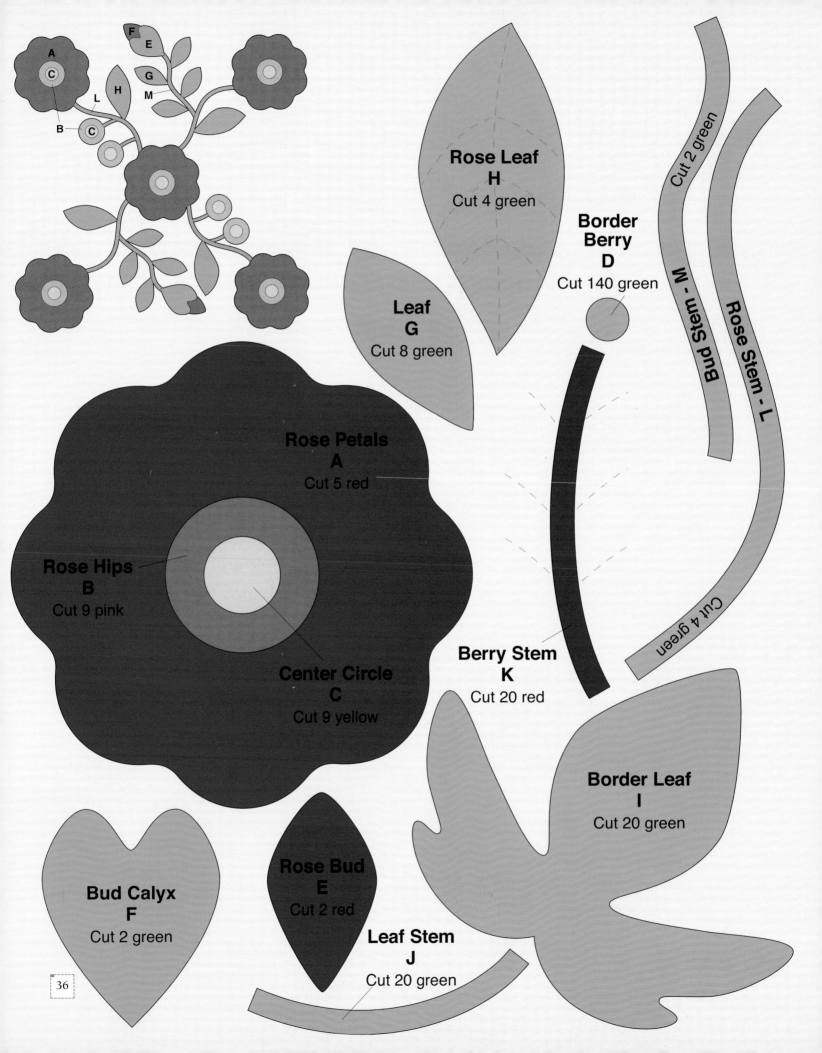

**Rose Leaf
H**
Cut 4 green

**Border
Berry
D**
Cut 140 green

**Leaf
G**
Cut 8 green

Cut 2 green

Bud Stem - M

Rose Stem - L

**Rose Petals
A**
Cut 5 red

**Rose Hips
B**
Cut 9 pink

**Center Circle
C**
Cut 9 yellow

**Berry Stem
K**
Cut 20 red

Cut 4 green

**Border Leaf
I**
Cut 20 green

**Bud Calyx
F**
Cut 2 green

**Rose Bud
E**
Cut 2 red

**Leaf Stem
J**
Cut 20 green

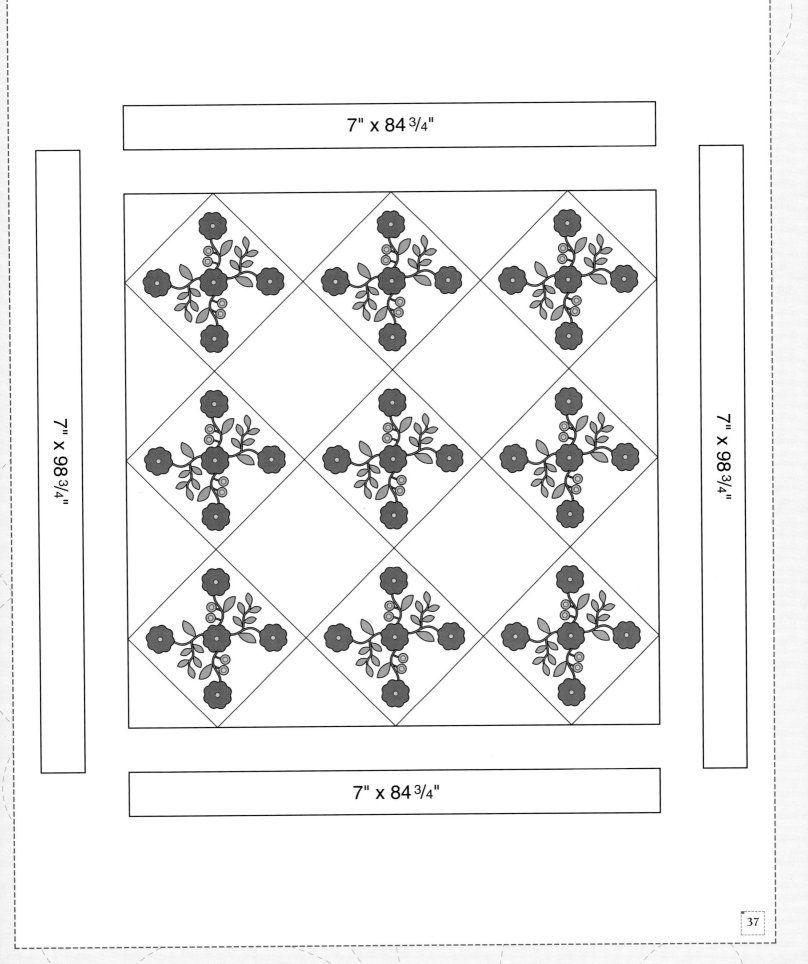

7" x 84 ³/₄"

7" x 98 ³/₄"

7" x 98 ³/₄"

7" x 84 ³/₄"

Sprouting Hearts and Berries
Susan Mary Wyant Beard Howerton (1831-1929)
87" x 87"
Collection of Ollideen S. Wright

Susan Mary Wyant was born in 1831 in Newcomerstown, Ohio. We do not know whether she made her Sprouting Hearts quilt in her native state, or in Kentucky, a possibility held by her descendants, or in Indiana where the family lived just before migrating to Kansas. In the early 1870s, Susan and her husband William J. Beard came to Kansas from Madison County, Indiana, by covered wagon with their four children Susan, George, Luella and Laura. William, a veteran of the Civil War (89th Indiana Regiment), died soon after their arrival. In 1874 Susan was married again to Lee Howerton, a neighbor with five children who had also lost his spouse. However, the 1880 census shows her as the head of her household, living on her own farm in Neosho County, Kansas, with her three youngest children. In later years she was keeper of the hotel in the small town of Stark. She died in 1929 at the age of 98. When Susan's great-granddaughter, Ollideen Wright, was a child in the 1920s, she was able to visit her by-then quite elderly great-grandmother. She remembers Susan picking wild strawberries, and further recalls that she was "never sick," that she walked to the grocery store every day, and that she "always wore those long full-skirted dresses made out of gingham." It is remarkable to think that since Susan was born in 1831 and her great-granddaughter still has personal memories of her in this year of 2006, this makes a connection spanning 175 years between these two women.

Susan's quilt illustrates the Germanic "sprouting heart" design. A large heart is the vessel from which stems a center sprouting flower, which in turn sprouts three stems and leaves. The heart shape is repeated on each stem. From each heart grows a cluster of berries. The quilt's sixteen blocks are framed by a narrow inner border of red and green pieced triangles and squares. An appliquéd meandering vine of grapes and leaves fills the wide, white outer border. Alternate white areas are quilted with feathered wreaths with grid centers. Half wreaths are positioned along the inside of the pieced inner border. Cross-hatch quilting fills the background of the outer border.

Log cabin; unknown woman holding baby

39

Sprouting Hearts
20" Finished
Stitched by Barb Fife

For 1 - 20" sampler block

Pattern pieces

A – Large heart, cut 1 red

B – Small heart, cut 3 red

C – Center rosette, cut 1 red

D – Leaf, cut 8 green

E – Small heart stem, cut 3, and 3 reverse red

F – Curved heart stems, cut 1, and 1 reverse, green (also used in border for green berries)

G – Large circle, cut 1 yellow for rosette. Cut 6 red for small heart B.

H – Berries, cut 39 red — 13 red berries for each small heart. Berries may be embroidered. (Option: Trace pattern H onto an Avery circle label, stick it onto the fabric, and cut around the circle.)

I – Border leaf, cut 40 green.

J – Stem, shown on page 44, cut a 1/2" x 3" red strip for a finished 1/4" x 2 1/2" stem. Embroider tiny stems on large stem. Cut 1 - 20 1/2" square for your background block. Set on square.

Sewing

* Place large heart, A, in corner of block. Pin.
* Pin 1/2" x 12" finished bias strip coming out of heart and placed on center fold line.
* Sew large circle G to center rosette C. Place and pin rosette on stem 5" from large heart.
* Place and pin stems F and FR coming out of rosette C. Refer to picture.
* Pin all green leaves D as shown.
* Prepare the berry stems, and all berries H. There are 13 berries per stem, 4 on each side of the stem, and 5 on the center stem. Embroider small stems on each side of the berry stem.
* Place small heart B on the end of the top and side stems, pin.
* Place E stems on B hearts and G berries on stem ends.
* Baste all pieces.
* Applique.

For large quilt 111" x 111"

For the original vintage quilt, I changed the size of the blocks to 16" finished. There are 16 appliquéd blocks and 9 plain blocks, all set on point with no sashing. The plain blocks give an opportunity for the lovely feather wreaths and elaborate designs that make these quilts so beautiful, whether quilted by hand or machine. The pieced border that surrounds the blocks is a simple 2 1/2" finished square in a square block in red and green. Complementing the sprouting hearts is a lovely appliquéd vine with leaves and green berries on appliquéd or embroidered stems. The vine is made with 1" finished bias strips, placed in a deep curve.

For setting blocks and triangle

* Cut 16 - 16 1/2" background squares for appliqué.
* Cut 9 - 16 1/2" squares for quilting designs, figure 1.
* Cut 3 - 23 7/8" squares, cut into 4 side triangles, figure 2.
* Cut 2 - 12 1/2" squares, on diagonal for corner triangles, figure 3.

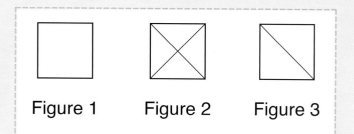

Figure 1   Figure 2   Figure 3

Quilting designs

- Choose a large feathered circle or repeat the appliqué patterns of hearts, stems, leaves and berries as your quilting design. Place a 1" square grid behind the appliqués to fill in the background.

Sewing pieced border

- Now, piece the 2 1/2" finished square in a square block. Make 26 for each side of the quilt plus 4 more blocks for the 4 corners for a total of 120 - 2 1/2" x 2 1/2" square blocks.
- Sew red and green squares into 4 rows for each side of quilt.
- For the corners, sew the 4 corner squares to each side of top and bottom rows. See figure 5.
- Quilt now measures 95 1/2" x 95 1/2".

For outside border

Complementing the sprouting hearts is a lovely appliquéd vine with leaves and green berries on appliquéd or embroidered stems. The vine is made with 1" finished bias strips, placed in a deep curve.

I – Border leaf, cut 40 green leaves
H – Berry, cut 11 green berries per stem, 440 total
F – Stem, cut 40 red stems for green berries
Red border vine is a 1" finished bias strip.

Appliquéd borders

See figure #5

- Cut top and bottom borders 8 1/2" x 95 1/2"
- Cut 2 side borders 8 1/2" x 111 1/2"
- Lay out prepared 1" bias stems, either by using the "Vine Line Tool" to mark the borders and corners, or lay out vine by eye following the picture. Pin and baste vine in place. You may want to lay out the vine first on each border, leaving a long tail to make the corner loop after borders are sewn to the quilt.
- Leaves, berries, and embroidered stems should be appliquéd and stitched onto the borders before the borders are sewn to quilt.

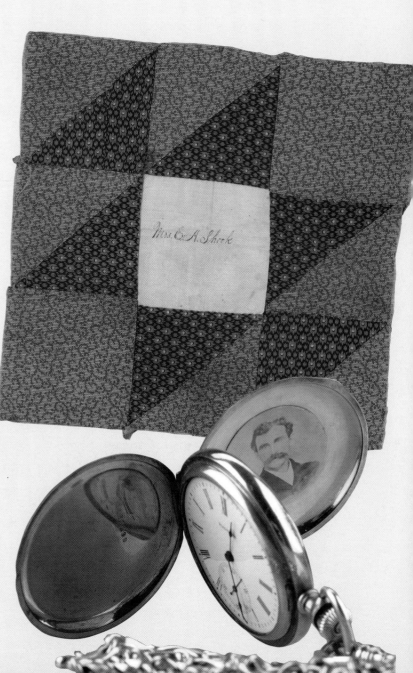

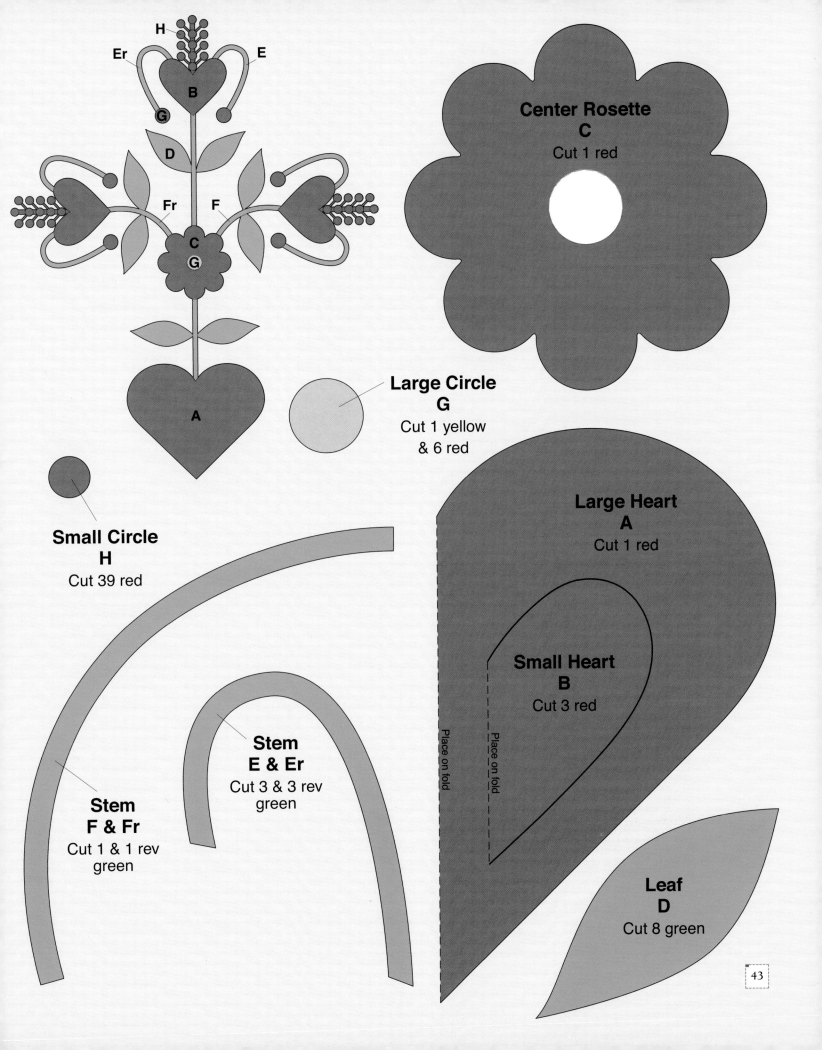

Center Rosette
C
Cut 1 red

Large Circle
G
Cut 1 yellow
& 6 red

Small Circle
H
Cut 39 red

Large Heart
A
Cut 1 red

Small Heart
B
Cut 3 red

Place on fold

Place on fold

Stem
E & Er
Cut 3 & 3 rev
green

Stem
F & Fr
Cut 1 & 1 rev
green

Leaf
D
Cut 8 green

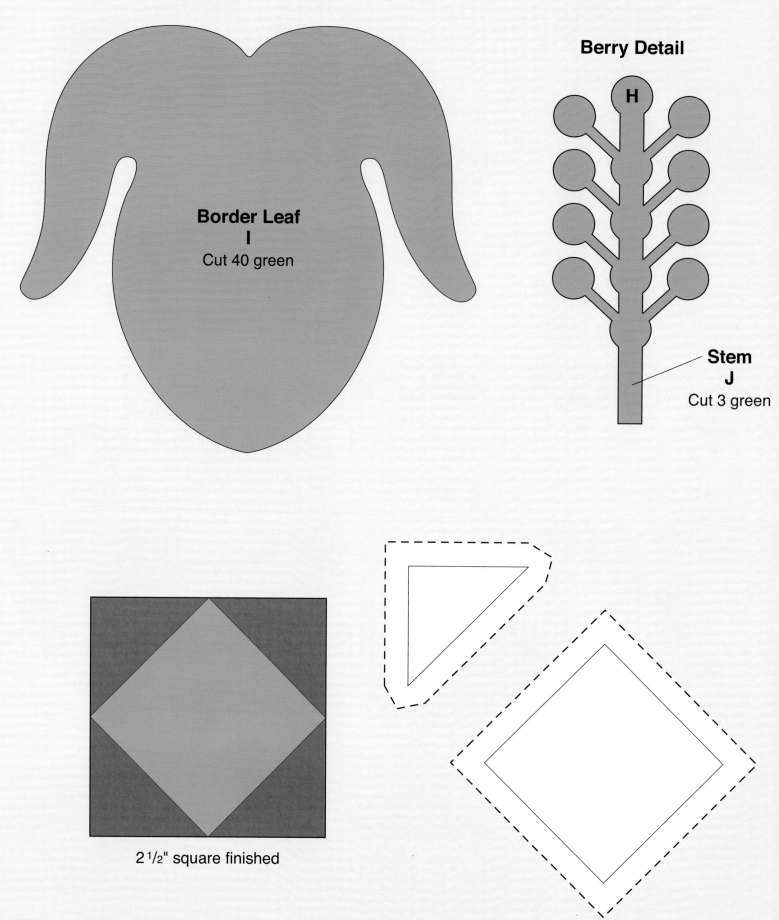

Border Leaf
I
Cut 40 green

Berry Detail

H

Stem
J
Cut 3 green

2 1/2" square finished

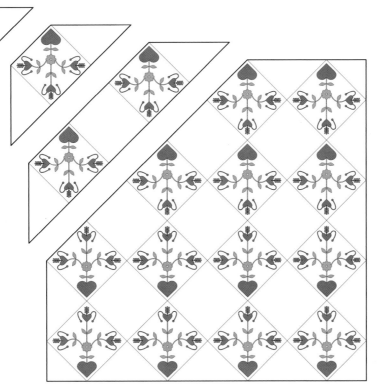

Figure 4

| 8 " x 95" |

2 ¹/₂" x 90 ¹/₂"

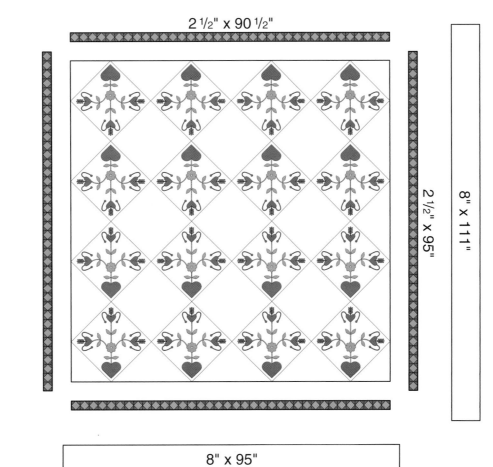

8" x 111"

2 ¹/₂" x 95"

8" x 111"

8" x 95"

Figure 5

Christmas Tulip
Rachel Elmira Roach White (1824-1890)
Made in Illinois, 1876. 64" x 81"
Collection of Sarah Godbey and Neva Jane Upp

Rachel Elmira Roach was born in Nashville, Tennessee, in 1824. She married Robert Franklin White in Morgan County, Illinois, in 1844. Rachel made the tulip quilt as a wedding present for her daughter, Esther Ann, when she married William T. Moore in 1876 on a farm near Petersburg in central Illinois. Esther and William bought a walnut bed, which was not new even then. It is still in use in the family and has now "slept six generations." The family calls the quilt "the Christmas quilt" and puts it on the antique bed every year to enjoy during the Advent and Christmas seasons. Esther White Moore, like her mother, made quilts. In 1926, she and William celebrated their golden wedding anniversary in Farmer City, Illinois.

Rachel Elmira Roach White, 1864.

On the Christmas Tulip quilt, straight stems of red tulips and green leaves radiate from a center pattern piece in a simple yet effective design. An undulating border vine holds stems of rosettes and buds in varying stages of bloom. The quilt contains six full blocks and three half blocks. The white background is quilted entirely in parallel diagonal lines. A row of half-blocks appears in the Christmas Tulip. Was this to fit a specific bed, or because the half-blocks would have been on the side of the bed that was against the wall and would not show? Or was it a matter of practicality, to save time, yardage and thread?

Descendants of Rachel White and Esther Moore still put the Tulip quilt on the antique walnut bed each Christmas.
Courtesy of Neva Jane Upp and Sarah Godbey

Christmas Tulip
20" Finished
Stitched by Barb Fife

For 1-20" sampler block

Pattern pieces

A – Tulip, cut 4 red

B – Center design, cut 1 green

C – Leaf, cut 8 green

D – Border rose bud, cut 15 red

E – Calyx for border rose bud, cut 15 green

F – Large border rose for borders, cut 17 red

G – Large calyx for border rose, cut 17 green

H – Large bud for borders, cut 17 red

I – Small calyx for borders, cut 17 green

J – Small bud for borders, cut 17 red

K – Stem for flowers and buds in the borders, cut 32 long, 1" wide bias strips

L – Border leaf, cut 39 green

    Cut 1 - 20 1/2" square for background block.

Sewing

- Place the 2 - 1/2" x 15 1/2" crossing stems M in the middle of the block. Pin and baste the following:
- Place center design B over the stems where they meet in the middle.
- Place tulip A, leaf C, as shown.
- Appliqué all pattern pieces.
- Set on square.

Quilt 70" x 80"

The original quilt has 6 full size blocks and 3 half blocks.

- Cut 6 - 20 1/2" squares of background fabric.
- Cut 3 - 10 1/2" x 20 1/2" rectangles for the 3 half blocks on the side of the quilt.
- Appliqué blocks following the instructions for the sampler block, except for the three half blocks. Cut pattern piece B just as it is on the pattern, but add 1/4" to the "place on fold" line so you have a seam allowance to turn.
  Set blocks as shown on page 52.

- Border vines are 1/2" bias strips that run off the edge of the top border and at the top of the 2 side borders. The 2 corner vines float across the seam lines of the 2 bottom corners.
- Follow the photo for placing the border tulips, rosettes, buds and leaves.
- Cut top and bottom borders 10 1/2" x 50 1/2".
- Cut 2 side borders 10 1/2" x 80 1/2".
- Follow the diagram on page 52 for border placement.

Needles and handmade leather thimble from the 19th century.

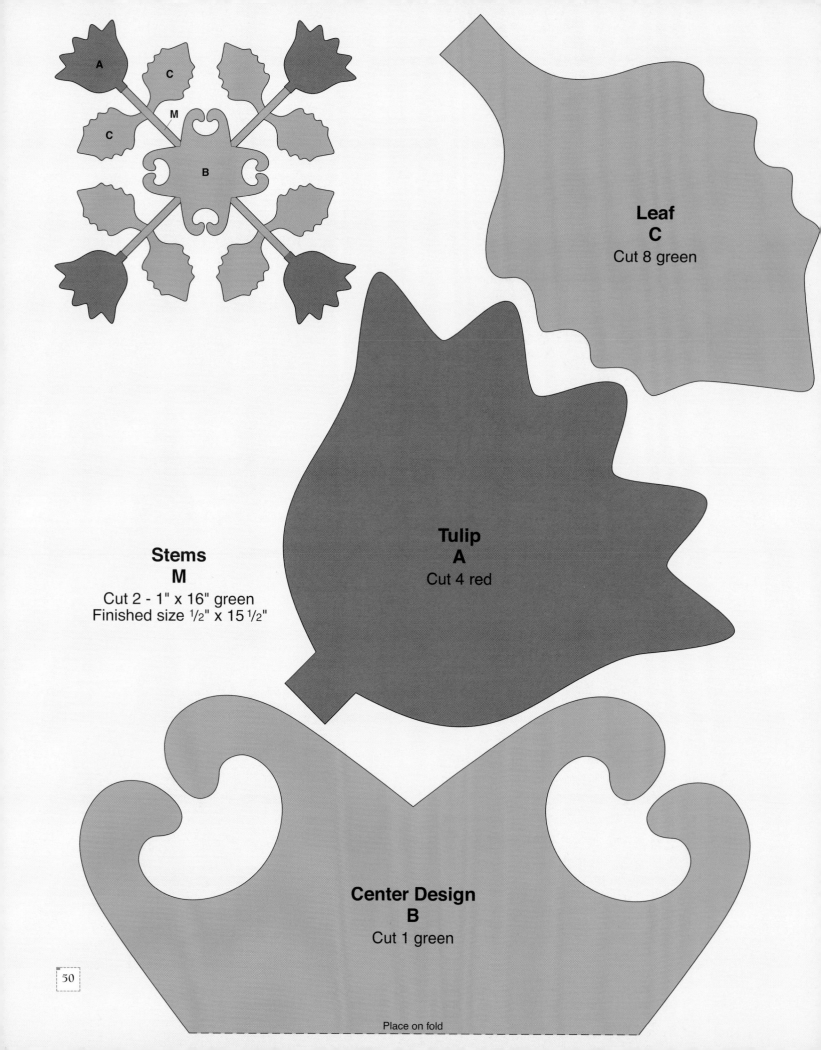

**Leaf
C**
Cut 8 green

**Stems
M**

Cut 2 - 1" x 16" green
Finished size 1/2" x 15 1/2"

**Tulip
A**
Cut 4 red

**Center Design
B**
Cut 1 green

Place on fold

Border Small Bud J
Cut 17 red

Border Small Calyx I
Cut 17 green

Border Rose Bud D
Cut 15 red

Border Stem K
Cut 32 green

Border Rose Bud Calyx E
Cut 15 green

Border Leaf L
Cut 39 green

Border Large Bud H
Cut 17 red

Large Border Rose F
Cut 17 red

Border Large Calyx G
Cut 17 green

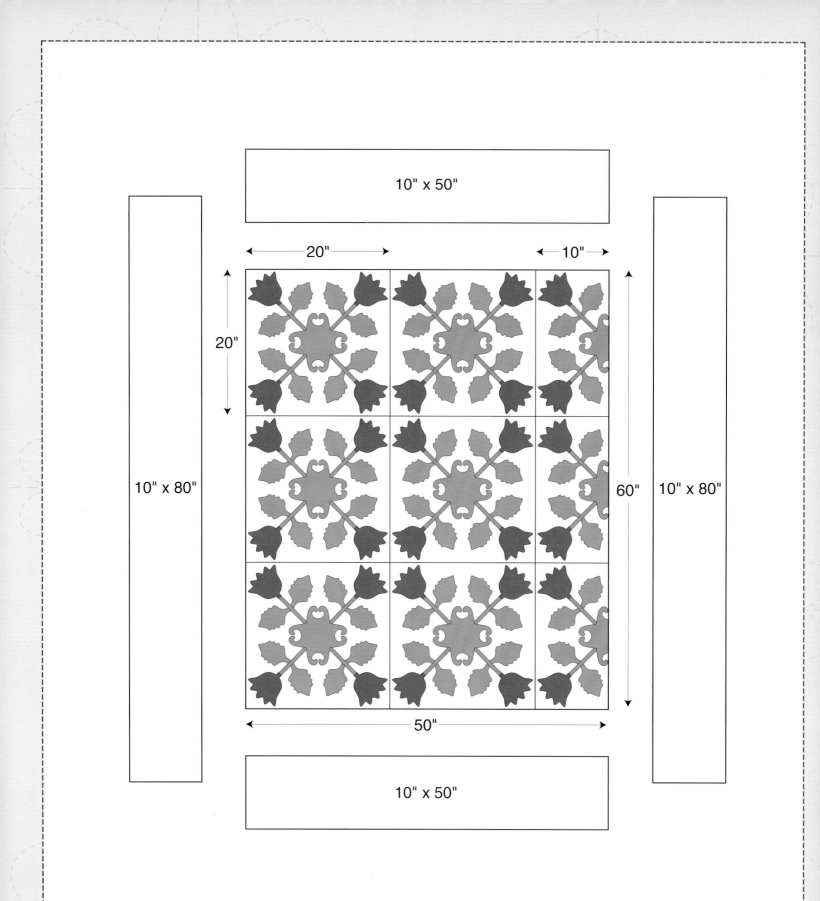

10" x 50"

20"   ← 10" →

20"

10" x 80"   60"   10" x 80"

50"

10" x 50"

He who does not appreciate floral beauty …
… is to pitied like any other man who
is born imperfect.

Sarah McCampbell's *Whig Rose*

Whig Rose
Sarah Elizabeth Bryan McCampbell (1857-1898)
Made in Tennessee. 61" x 81"
Collection of Georgia Hindman

Sarah Elizabeth Bryan was born in Tennessee in 1857, the daughter of Margaret Callahan and Ahaz Bryan. When she was a child during the Civil War, according to a story from her grandson David McCampbell, she was said to be taking food to troops near her home when she was struck by a stray bullet fired by a Union soldier that ricocheted and shot her in the leg ("damn Yankee shot her.") She limped all her life. Her grandchildren also report that Sarah smoked a pipe.

Sarah married David P. McCampbell in 1879. They lived in Sevier County, Tennessee, and were parents of ten children. Sarah died in 1898, and in 1902 David moved to Kansas to make a new home with his eight surviving children: Nora 20, Lucy 18, Walter 16, Kate 14, Maggie 12, Beecher 11, Alec 8, and Ted, just three years old.

In a memoir titled *Chronicles of the McCampbell Family in Kansas*, granddaughter Bonnie McCampbell Flynn writes that in addition to their household possessions "each child was allowed one satchel or traveling bag to carry personal special things, and each child also carried a slip of some kind of plant indigenous to Tennessee. Lucy … brought some boxwood, others … chose [sic] fruit tree seedlings, whatever was their choice…" Some of the pear trees they planted are still on the old Kansas farm today.

David McCampbell homesteaded a quarter section of land near Fowler, Kansas. He built a dugout there and "proved up" the land. Properties to the north and west were claimed by Maggie, Kate, Lucy and Beecher. Each young person upon the age of eighteen, even the females, claimed a quarter section to homestead.

Instead of the curved stems usually found on 19th century Whig Rose patterns, Sarah McCampbell chose to vary hers by making the stems of her roses stiff and straight. The center designs are also unique, made up of eight-pointed green and yellow stars surrounded by red and yellow wedge-shaped pieces. The top and bottom borders are banded with stripes of red, green, and yellow. Parallel lines and cross-hatch quilting fill the background.

Sarah Elizabeth Bryan McCampbell.
Courtesy of Georgia Hindman

McCampbell dugout in western Kansas.
Courtesy of Bonnie Flynn McCampbell

David and Sarah McCampbell's home in Tennessee.
Courtesy of Bonnie Flynn McCampbell

55

Whig Rose
20" Finished
Stitched by Barb Fife

For 1 - 20" sampler block

Pattern Pieces

A – Roses, cut 8 red

B – Rose calyx, cut 16 green

C – Stem and calyx, cut 4 green

D – Bud, cut 4 red

E – Calyx, cut 4 yellow

F – Rose crowns, cut 4 red

G – Leaf, cut 20 green

    Stem, cut 2 – 1/2" x 18" for roses, and

    4 – 1 1/2" x 8" stems for buds

a – Circle, cut 1 red

b – Star ray, cut 8 yellow

c – Star piece, cut 8 green

    Cut 1 - 20 1/2" square for background block

Sewing

- Assemble units of four buds E-D-C.
- Assemble units of roses A and rose calyx B.
- Piece the center circle star with pieced patterns a-b-c. This unit will be different from the original quilt. I made it a little smaller to fit the 20" block.
- Place 8 stems around the pieced center. Pin and baste.
- Pin and baste rose and bud units on stems, refer to picture for placement.
- Place large rose crown as shown with tips under the center star circle.
- Pin and baste leaves G as shown in picture.
- Place pieced star unit over ends of stems and crowns in the middle of the block. Pin and baste.

For the quilt 72" x 90"

- For the original 4-block quilt, the blocks measure a 36" x 36" square. Cut four background blocks 36 1/2" x 36 1/2". Use the larger templates for appliqués to fit the bigger squares.
- Also add four more bud units (E-D-C) and square to sew to intersecting center seams, and place the 3" square on point over the ends of the bud units.
- For striped borders see diagram on page 61.

A similar block from Terry's collection

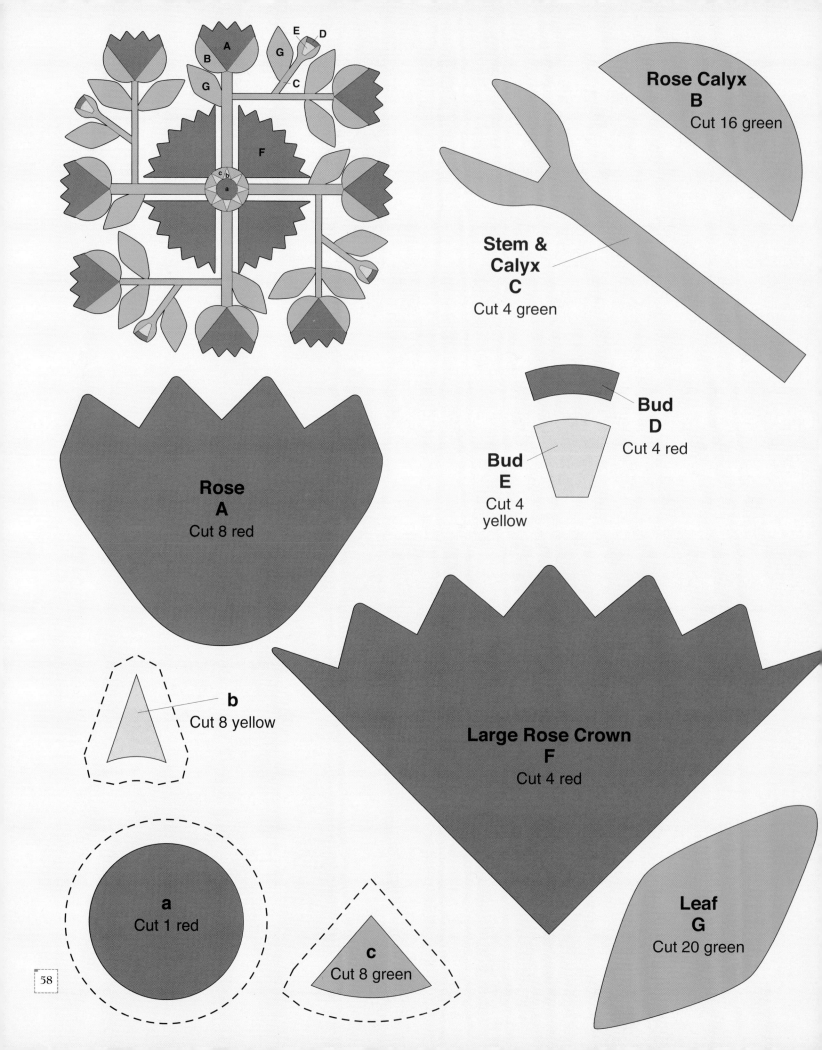

Rose Calyx
B
Cut 16 green

Stem &
Calyx
C
Cut 4 green

Bud
D
Cut 4 red

Bud
E
Cut 4
yellow

Rose
A
Cut 8 red

b
Cut 8 yellow

Large Rose Crown
F
Cut 4 red

a
Cut 1 red

c
Cut 8 green

Leaf
G
Cut 20 green

Templates for 36" blocks

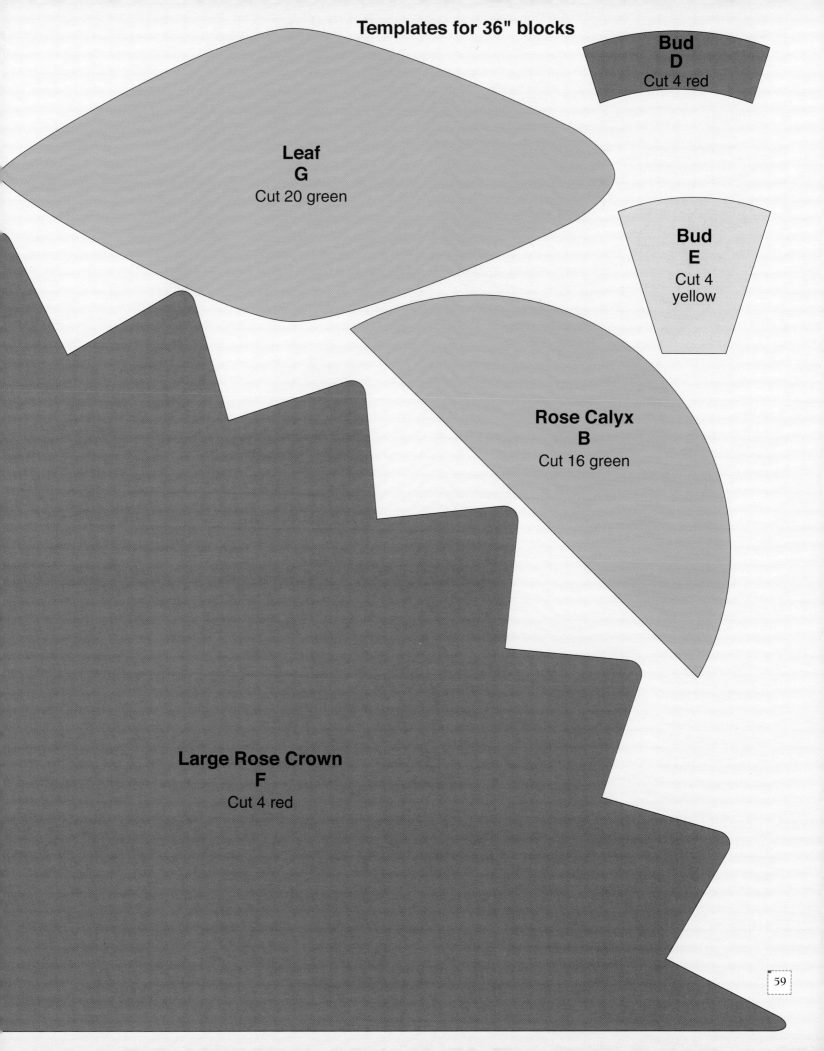

Bud
D
Cut 4 red

Leaf
G
Cut 20 green

Bud
E
Cut 4
yellow

Rose Calyx
B
Cut 16 green

Large Rose Crown
F
Cut 4 red

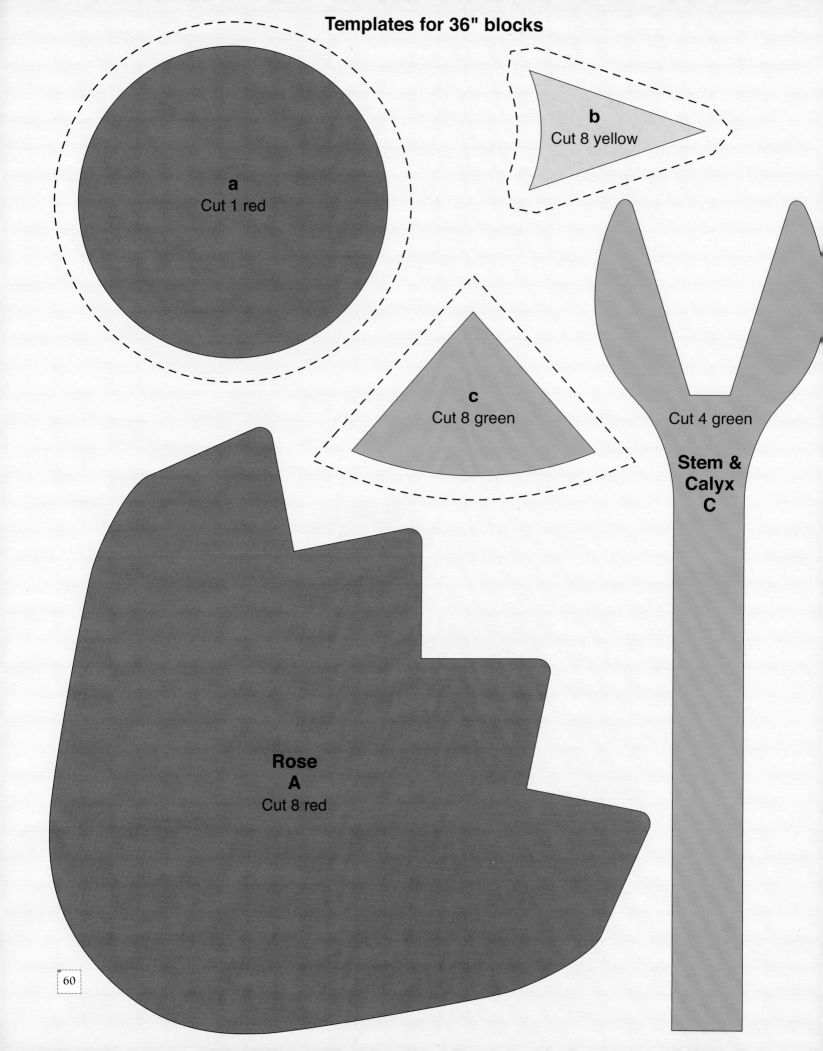

Templates for 36" blocks

a
Cut 1 red

b
Cut 8 yellow

c
Cut 8 green

Cut 4 green

Stem & Calyx C

Rose A
Cut 8 red

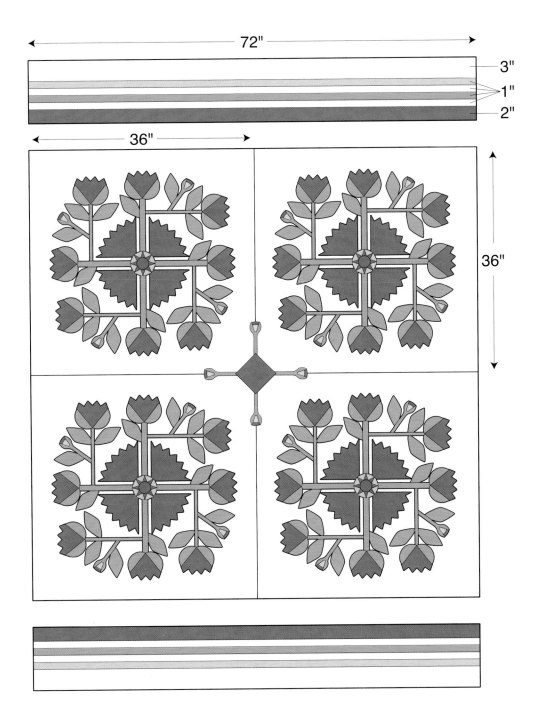

Figure 1

Pennsylvania Tulips
Rebecca Baughman Wilhelm
Made in Kansas, 1895. 86" x 89"
Collection of Lois Coberly

Rebecca Baughman was born in Ohio in 1837. She married Thomas Wilhelm, a native Pennsylvanian and a lumberman. Shortly before 1870 they moved their growing family to Emporia, Kansas. Rebecca made this quilt for her daughter Celia's wedding to Edward Gunkel on December 25, 1895. Celia and Edward's son John grew up to marry the grandniece of Isabel Andrews. (See page 33).

Rebecca Wilhelm's quilt is a variation of the vase and flowers design in which the vase has been replaced by a small triangular shape. A tulip in red and chrome orange is on a long slender center stem. The tulip is repeated on two symmetrical side stems. The placement of the blocks, set diagonally in a staggered arrangement, gives the quilt an interesting overall composition. The background behind the tulips is entirely quilted in straight lines. Wide, plain white borders are filled with quilted feather

sprays. The quilt is edged with tan piping, sewn next to the binding. This was unusual for a quilt made in the latter part of the 1800s; it was a technique more common several decades earlier. In this quilt, the green fabric has faded to tan. Synthetic dyes at the end of the 19th century were not reliable; they faded quickly when exposed to sunlight and harsh laundry. The red, tan, and white colors are typical of quilts made in the red and green appliqué style in the late 1800s.

Sign, "McCall's – Patterns for 15¢."

Turn of the 20th century, unknown woman in dry goods store doing needlework.

Tulip design on a coverlet. The Daughters of the American Revolution Museum, Washington, D.C. Gift of Caroline Garberich Howard, in honor of Mary Leatherman Means.

Pennsylvania Tulips
20" Finished
Stitched by Barb Fife

For 1 - 20" sampler block

Pattern pieces

A – Vase, cut 1 green

B– Tulip petals, cut 3 red and 3 reverse

C – Center tulip petal, cut 3 gold

D – Calyx, cut 3 green, and 3 reverse

E – Tulip leaves, cut 2 green and 2 reverse

F – Stems, cut 1 green and 1 reverse

Center stem, cut 1 green 1" x 12 1/2"

Sewing

- Place triangle vase in corner of block or in center, whichever you prefer. Pin and baste.
- Place finished 1/2" x 12 1/2" center stem in the middle of vase. Pin and baste.
- Place side stems F and Fr on either side of center stem. Pin and baste.
- Sew 3 tulip units C, B, Br, and calyx D & Dr.
- Place tulip units on end of curved stems and center stem. Pin and baste.
- Place leaves E and ER in vase as shown in picture, and on center stem.
- Appliqué all pieces.

For the quilt 84 3/4" x 104 3/4"

- Cut 13 - 20 1/2" squares for background blocks.
- Cut 2 - 29 5/8" squares, cut into 4 triangles (figure # 1) for 8 setting triangles.
- Cut 2 - 15 1/8" squares, cut into 4 triangles for corners (figure #2).

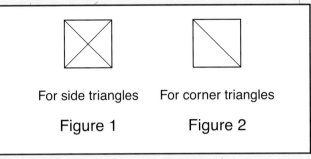

For side triangles   For corner triangles

Figure 1   Figure 2

- Follow figure #3 for setting blocks, triangles and corners.
- Cut top and bottom borders 10 1/2" x 85 1/4".
- Cut 2 side borders 10 1/2" x 105 1/2".
- Sew top and bottom borders to quilt, then sew the side borders. See figure #4.
- Quilt block background in 1" parallel lines.

Outline each appliqué piece. Choose the pattern from the quilting section that looks like an open feather that is the "standing feather" on page 98 for the borders.

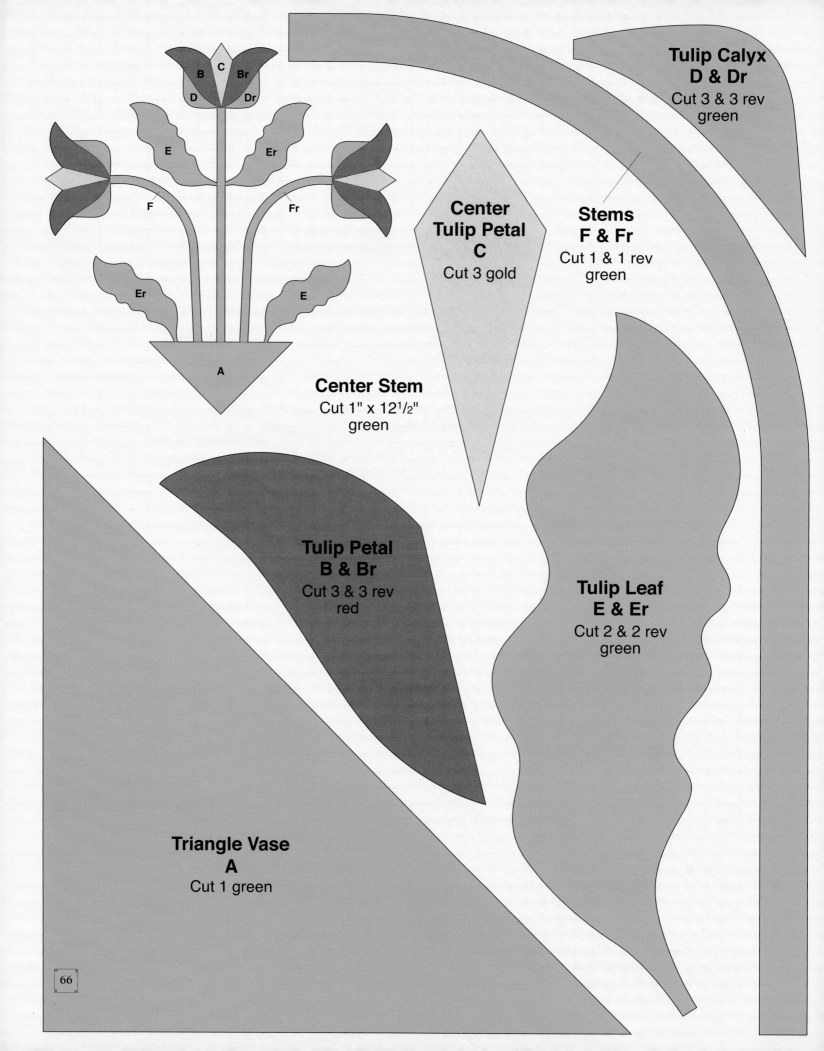

**Tulip Calyx
D & Dr**

Cut 3 & 3 rev
green

**Center
Tulip Petal
C**

Cut 3 gold

**Stems
F & Fr**

Cut 1 & 1 rev
green

Center Stem

Cut 1" x 12$\frac{1}{2}$"
green

**Tulip Petal
B & Br**

Cut 3 & 3 rev
red

**Tulip Leaf
E & Er**

Cut 2 & 2 rev
green

**Triangle Vase
A**

Cut 1 green

Figure 3

10" x 84 3/4"

10" x 104 3/4"

10" x 104 3/4"

10" x 84 3/4"

Figure 4

Lydia's Garden Quilt
Lydia Marie Erwin Mason (1840-1916)
Made in Illinois, 1860. 64" x 74"
Collection of Jacqualine Byers Frisbie

Lydia Marie Erwin was born near Zanesville, Ohio, in 1840. Family tradition holds that Lydia made her quilt about 1860. In 1866 she married Amos L. Mason at Ottawa, Illinois, after he was discharged from the 104th Illinois Infantry. The Masons lived in the Streator, Illinois, area for a time; in 1868 they moved to Missouri, and in 1880 moved again to Smith County, Kansas. There they established a homestead and built a four room rock house, with two rooms downstairs and two rooms upstairs.

Lydia's unusual quilt has five blocks set on point. Each block has two main stems that start at the bottom of the block and cross to opposing corners. The third stem extends toward the top corner. The flower is composed of a center rosette with a circle in the middle of the rosette. The first row is red; the second row is made up of eight orange teardrops, and the third consists of eight red teardrops. Encircling each rosette are eight leaves that alternate with the last row of teardrops. Triangles surrounding the five blocks are each filled with one bloom and one stem.

Amos and Lydia Marie Erwin Mason, c. 1866

"The Little Stone House," built by the Masons c. 1880 in Smith County, Kansas

Silk dress, Civil War era

Garden Quilt
20" Finished
Stitched by Barb Fife

For 1 - 20" sampler block

Pattern Pieces

A – Rosette, cut 3 red
B – Petal, cut 24 yellow/gold
C – Petal, cut 21 red
D – Center, cut 3 yellow/gold
E – Small rosette center, cut 2 yellow/gold
F – Small rosette, cut 2 red
G – Small leaf, cut 32 green
H – Large leaf, cut 1 green and 1 reverse
   Stems, cut 1" bias strips into 2 long lengths,
   turn edges with a 1/2" Clover bias maker.
   Cut 1 - 20 1/2" square for background block.

Sewing

Place appliqués on square.

- Place circle D on rosettes A for 3 flower units. Place and baste petals in between rosettes as shown.
- Lay out long finished 18" bias strips starting in left bottom corner. Follow picture for layout. Trim what you don't need.
- Arrange flowers on ends of stems, then arrange leaves G around flower heads and on stems. Pin and baste.
- Place 2-4" stems that hold the 2 small rosettes E/F.
- Pin and baste large leaves H on stems just above small rosettes.
- Appliqué all pieces.

For the large quilt 68" x 68"

Cutting and sewing blocks

- Cut 5 – 24 1/2" squares for the background blocks.
- Make 15 flowers with A, B & D for the 5 blocks on point, and make 8 flowers for the 4 corners and for the 4 setting triangles.
- Appliqué.

Setting triangles

- Small leaf G, cut 12
- Green leaf H, cut 4
- Cut 4 long stems
- Cut 2 – 35 1/2" squares. Cut on diagonal twice. See figure #1, page 73.

Corner triangles

- For 4 corner triangles, cut 2 – 17 7/8" squares. Cut once on the diagonal. See figure #2. Follow figures #3 and #4 for setting into the quilt.

There are five blocks on point, with setting triangles and corners, and no borders, but if you wish, add a chintz or calico border to enlarge and frame the quilt. Lydia was very "relaxed" about where she placed the flowers, stems and leaves in the setting triangles. That's one reason we like this quilt. Just lay in the designs you like and sew your own arrangement.

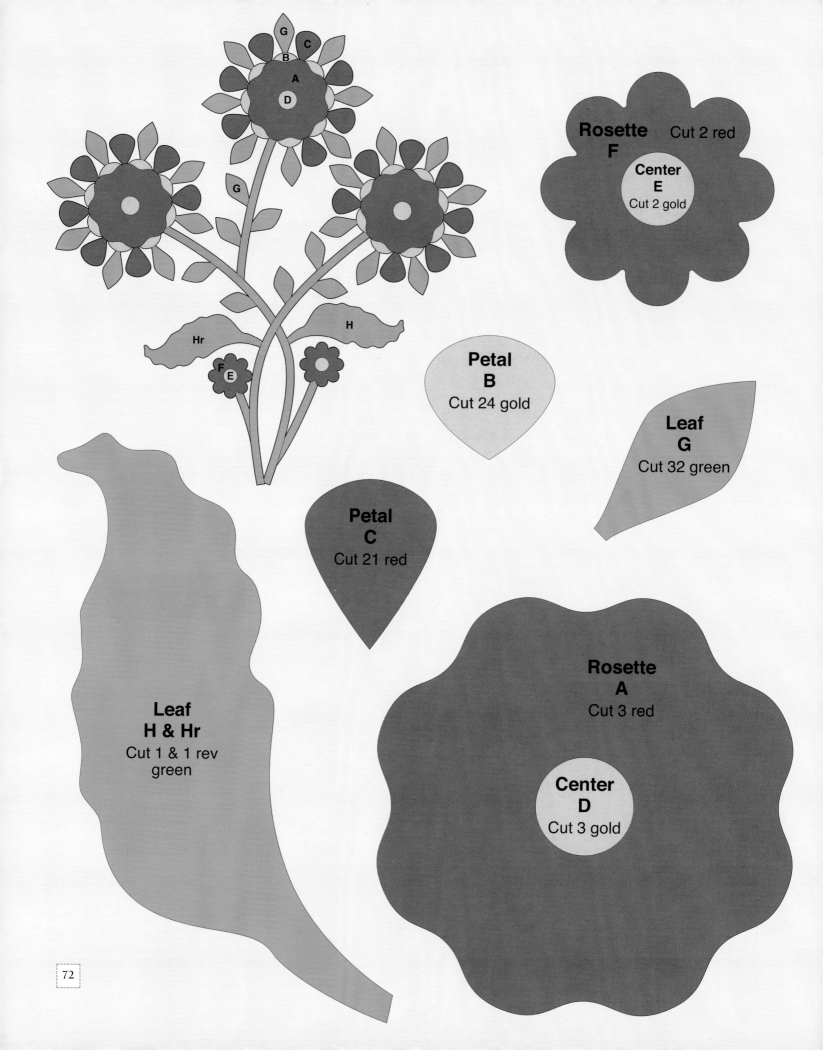

Rosette F Cut 2 red

Center E Cut 2 gold

Petal B Cut 24 gold

Leaf G Cut 32 green

Petal C Cut 21 red

Leaf H & Hr Cut 1 & 1 rev green

Rosette A Cut 3 red

Center D Cut 3 gold

Figure 3

Figure 4

Fig. #1

Fig. #2

Pomegranate and Thistle
Attributed to Queen City Methodist Quilters
80" x 82"
Collection of Nancy Hornback

This quilt came with a story that it was made by the Queen City, Missouri, Methodist quilters for the 25th wedding anniversary of Henry and Francis Barr Brenizer, and that the fabric for the quilt was purchased at Charley Sweeney's Dry Goods Store in Queen City. The 1870 census reveals that Henry was born about 1838 and Francis about 1842, both in Ohio. They were married in 1863 in Morrow County, Ohio, a date that would put their 25th anniversary in 1888. However, the style, fabrics and techniques of the quilt make us think it surely was made before this date. The embroidered buttonhole stitching in particular suggests an earlier time in the 19th century. We are speculating that perhaps the top was made by Francis Brenizer before her 1863 marriage and might have been quilted for her 25th wedding anniversary by the Queen City Methodist Quilters. If so, the reference to Charley Sweeney's Dry Goods Store could mean that the batting and backing were purchased there. We continue to investigate!

There are nine blocks in the quilt. A red feathered wreath is appliquéd in the center block. Pomegranates are in the four corner blocks. In the middle of each pomegranate is a reverse appliqué center of chrome yellow. Four blocks with appliquéd thistles are between the pomegranates. Four sunwheel designs cover the intersecting blocks' seam lines. The reverse buttonhole stitch is embroidered with cotton sewing thread around the raw edges of some of the appliqué pieces. Other pieces are appliquéd by turning under edges and securing them with a top running stitch. The thistle blooms are of one piece of red fabric, and the details of the petals are defined by button-hole stitching. In the quilt's border is a vine featuring a lily and a tulip, with details again filled in by the reverse buttonhole stitch. The reverse buttonhole stitch was not commonly found in appliqué, but we have discovered a few unique quilts that did use it to secure the appliqué pieces. See the photos on page 87.

Quilting on the Pomegranate and Thistle quilt consists of feather wreaths and quarter wreaths in the white spaces, filled in with half-inch diagonal parallel lines behind the appliquéd designs. Feathers are quilted along the border vine, and a full feather wreath is quilted around each sunwheel.

Group of women with tulip quilt in frame. Kansas State Historical Society.

Rendering by 20th Century Artist, Pennsylvania German dower chest. Image © National Gallery of Art, Washington, D.C.

Pomegranate
20" Finished
Stitched by Barb Fife

For 1-20" pomegranate sampler block

Pattern pieces
A – Pomegranate center, cut 1 red
B – Pomegranate middle, cut 1 yellow
C – Pomegranate outside, cut 1 red
D – Outer leaf, cut 1 red
E – Bud calyx, cut 3 green
F – Bud, cut 3 red
G – Bottom leaf, cut 1, and 1 reverse, green
   For stems, cut and finish 1/2" green bias strips
   for 1/4" finished stems for the pomegranate and
   thistle blocks. Cut into 7 1/2" lengths for the
   thistle stems holding buds. Use 5 1/2" lengths
   for 36 border stems for tulips and lilies.
   Cut 1-20 1/2" square for background block.

Sewing
*   Prepare the pomegranate pieces by first basting
    under the 1/4" seam allowance of the INSIDE
    edge of B and C.
*   Pin A in center of block, then lay the prebasted
    pieces B and C around A. Pin and baste.
*   Next pin and baste outer leaf D around bottom
    of pomegranate.
*   Assemble 3 buds F, and 3 calyx E, placing them
    around the pomegranate. Follow the picture for
    placement. Pin and baste.
*   Place finished 1/4" x 7 1/2" stems under
    pomegranate.
*   Add the bottom leaf G on either side of
    the stem.
*   Appliqué in a running stitch or a blind stitch.

For the 20" feather wreath sampler block

Pattern pieces
Cut 1 red 18" square for wreath.
Cut 1-20 1/2" square for background.

Sewing
*   Trace wreath pattern onto red square.
*   Cut out with a scant 1/8" seam allowance, as
    there is a very narrow space between the
    feathers. Appliqué with a reverse buttonhole
    stitch or a running or blind stitch.
*   Pin and baste in center of the 20 1/2" block.
    Baste through the middle of each feather and in
    the spine of the wreath.
*   The maker of this quilt hand-appliquéd this
    block with a top running stitch, using white
    thread. Besides being fast and practical, she
    worked at SHOWING her nice even stitches,
    not hiding them. See page 87.

For 1-20" thistle sampler block

Pattern pieces
A – Thistle bloom, cut 1 and 1 reverse, red
B – Bud #1, cut 1 green
C – Lower part of bud #1, cut 1 yellow
D – Calyx for bud #1, cut 1 green
E – Bud #2, cut 2 red
F – Calyx for bud #2, cut 2 green
G – Small leaf, cut 1 red for right side of thistle
   bud #1
H – Small leaf, cut 1 green for left side of thistle
   bud #1
I – Large leaf, cut 1 and 1 reverse, green
J – Medium leaf, cut 2 and 2 reverse, green
   Stems, 1 - 7 1/2" finished 1/2" bias stem, and
   2 - 5 1/2" finished 1/2" bias stems.
   Cut 1 - 20 1/2" square for background.

Thistle
20" Finished
Stitched by Barb Fife

Sewing (thistle block)

- Assemble center #1 bud, B, C, D calyx. Appliqué this unit. The maker used reverse buttonhole stitch (page 87).
- Place thistle bud unit in center of block, pin and baste
- Cut 1, reverse 1 of red thistle bloom. Place over each raw edge of center bud B. Appliqué to the bud unit.
- Place top small leaves, red G on the right and small green leaf H on the left. Pin and baste in place.
- Place 1 - 7 1/2" finished 1/4" bias stem under thistle.
- Place 2 - 5 1/2" finished 1/2" bias stems on center stem following the picture on page 78 for placement.
- Assemble 2 buds E with the calyx F.
- Place at ends of 5 1/2" stems.
- Place medium leaves J on 5 1/2" stems.
- Place large leaves I on each side of the main stem.

For large quilt

Make 1 feather wreath block, 4 pomegranate blocks, and 4 thistle blocks. (This unique quilt contains 3 lovely blocks, the feather wreath, the thistle, and a pomegranate. You may want to put all three blocks into your sampler quilt or choose the one you like best.)

For borders of large quilt

Pattern Piece list
A – Border lily, cut 16 red
B – Border tulip calyx, cut 16 green
C – Border tulip, cut 16 red
D – Sun wheel, cut 4 whole and 8 half, red
E – Center of sun wheel, cut 12 yellow
F – Border leaf, cut 32 green

- Cut top and bottom borders 10 1/2" x 60 1/2".
- Cut 2 side borders 10 1/2" x 80 1/2".

Sewing

Follow figure on page 84 for block placement, and borders.

- Optional: Applique 4 sun wheels over center seams, quilt edges and corners. See picture.
- For border vine, make long 2" green, bias strips for a 1" finished border vine. Pin and baste in deep curves.
- Use the Vine Line tool for making the borders or use the templates on pages 85 and 86. If you use the Vine Line tool, deep curve, line 1 works the best. Lay vine on border by eye.
- Place lilies and tulips, and leaves along 1" border vine. Pin and baste.
- Applique in a running or blind stitch, and in a reverse buttonhole stitch in the details of tulips and lilies. See photos on page 87. Follow the picture of corners and borders.

Quilting Patterns

- The Queen City quilters quilted double feather wreaths around the 4 sun wheels, and half wreaths around the 1/2 sun wheels on the edge of blocks.
- They filled in the backgrounds of the appliquéd blocks with diagonal straight lines 1/2" apart. See the quilt design section.
- On the border, feathers follow the curved vine on both sides, and are filled in again with the diagonal straight lines.

**Pom Center
A**
Cut 1 red

Place on fold

**Pom
Outside
C**
Cut 1 red

**Pom
Middle
B**
Cut 1 yellow

Place on fold

Place on fold

**Bottom
Leaf
G & Gr**
Cut 1 &
1 rev green

**Pom Bud
F**
Cut 3 red

**Bud Calyx
E**
Cut 3 green

**Pom Outer Leaf
D**
Cut 1 red

80

Place on fold

Thistle Bud #1
B
Cut 1 green

Thistle Calyx for Bud #1
C
Cut 1 yellow

Thistle Bloom A & Ar
Cut 1 & 1 rev red

Thistle Calyx for Bud #1
D
Cut 1 green

Medium Thistle Leaf J & Jr
Cut 2 & 2 rev green

Large Thistle Leaf I & Ir
Cut 1 & 1 rev green

Thistle Bud #2
E
Cut 2 red

Small Thistle Leaf H
Cut 1 green

Thistle Calyx for Bud #2
F
Cut 2 green

Cut 1 red

Small Thistle Leaf G

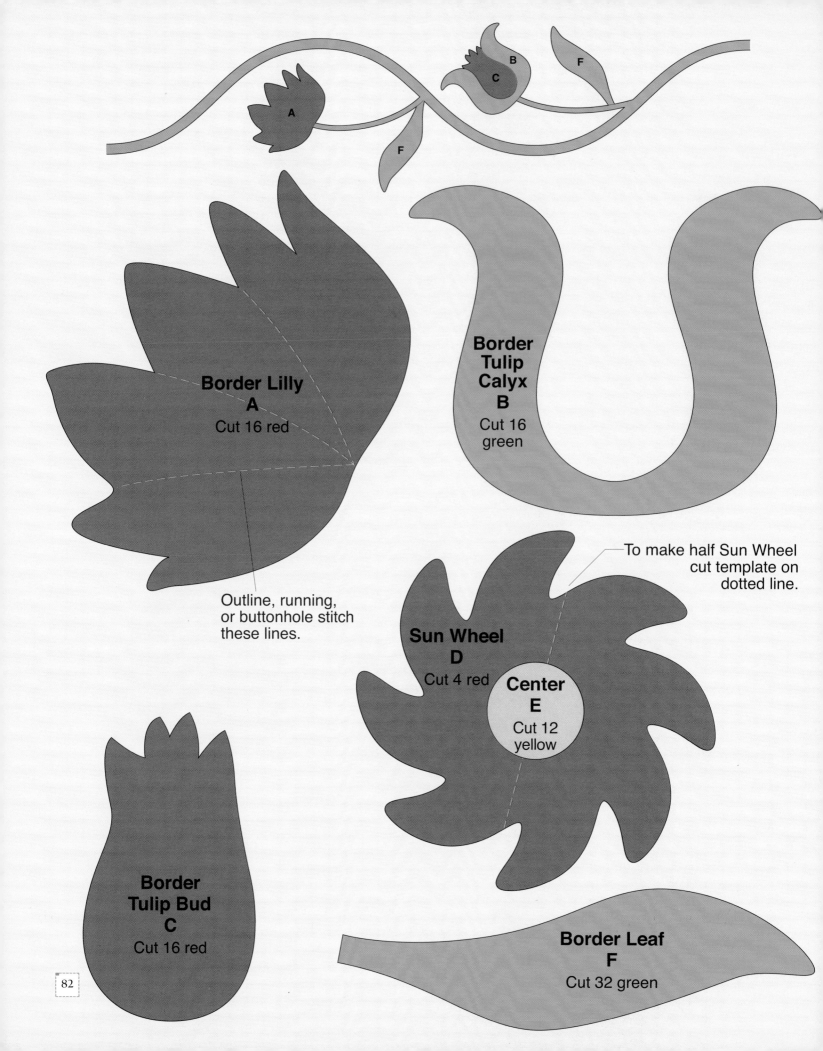

Border Lilly
A

Cut 16 red

Border
Tulip
Calyx
B

Cut 16
green

To make half Sun Wheel
cut template on
dotted line.

Outline, running,
or buttonhole stitch
these lines.

Sun Wheel
D

Cut 4 red

Center
E

Cut 12
yellow

Border
Tulip Bud
C

Cut 16 red

Border Leaf
F

Cut 32 green

Make 4 copies of template
and tape together as shown
to make full sized template.

**Feathered
Wreath**

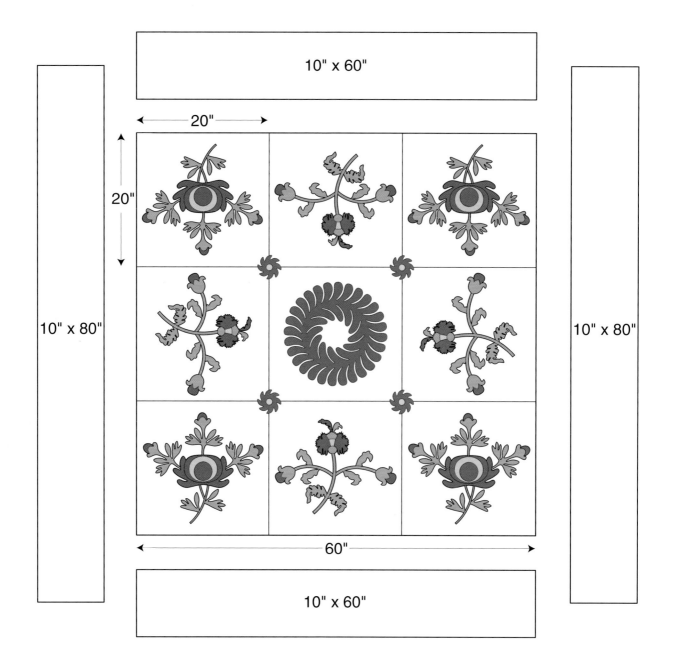

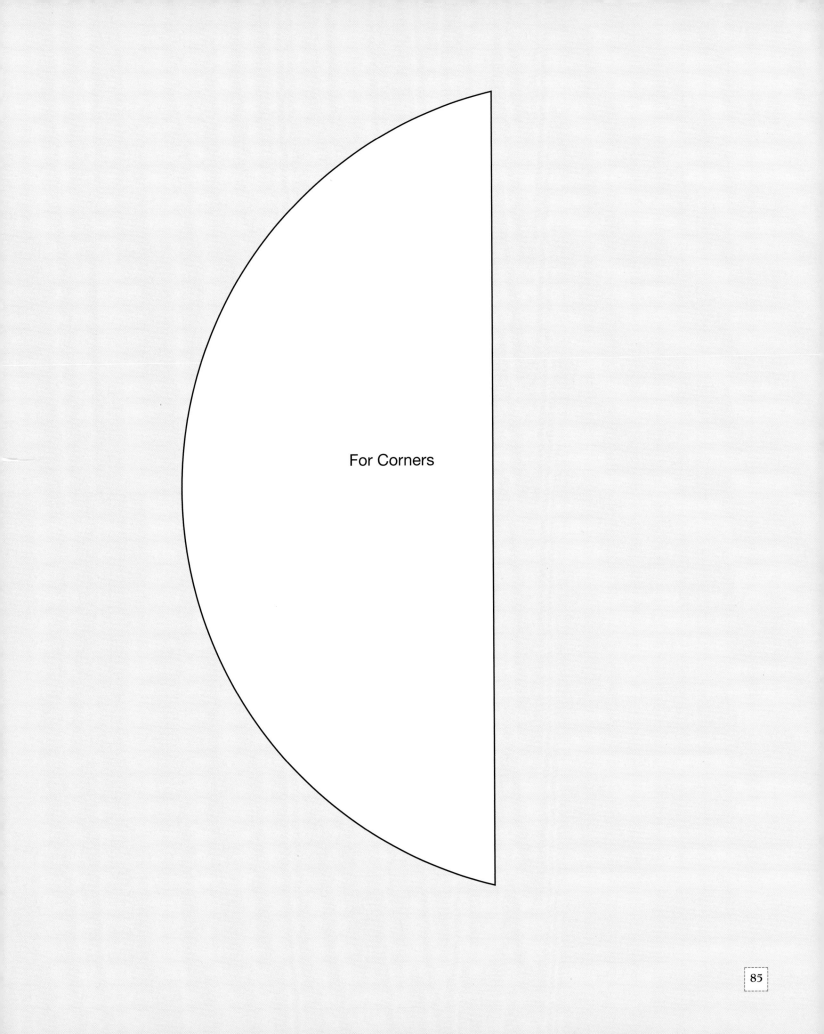

For Corners

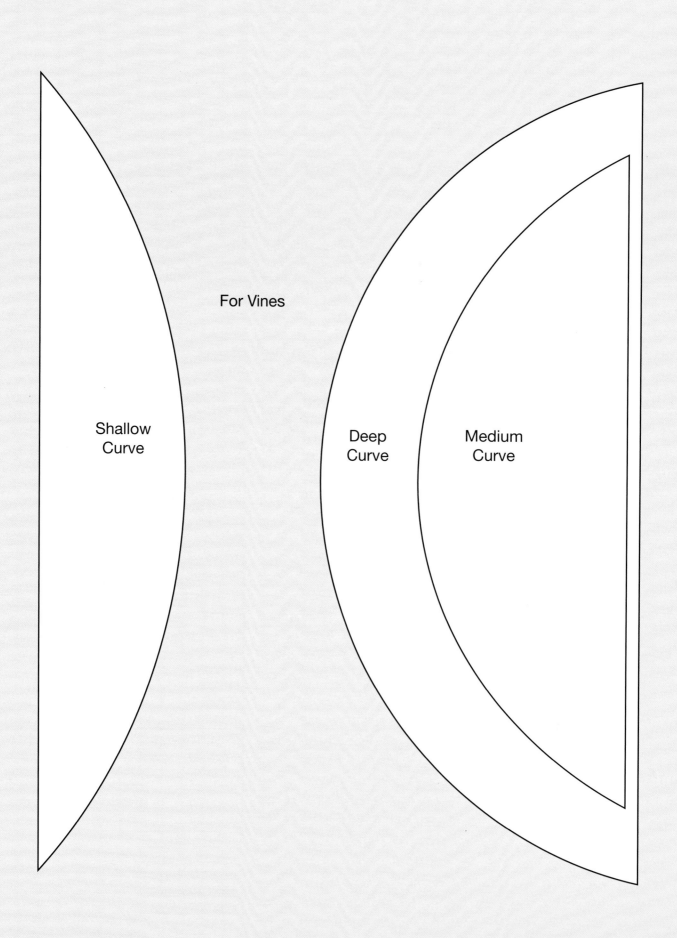

For Vines

Shallow
Curve

Deep
Curve

Medium
Curve

Templates and Quilting Patterns

Patterns from the original 19th century
quilts in this book, and some from
Nancy's and Terry's collection of
old patterns.

Seam line

Seam line

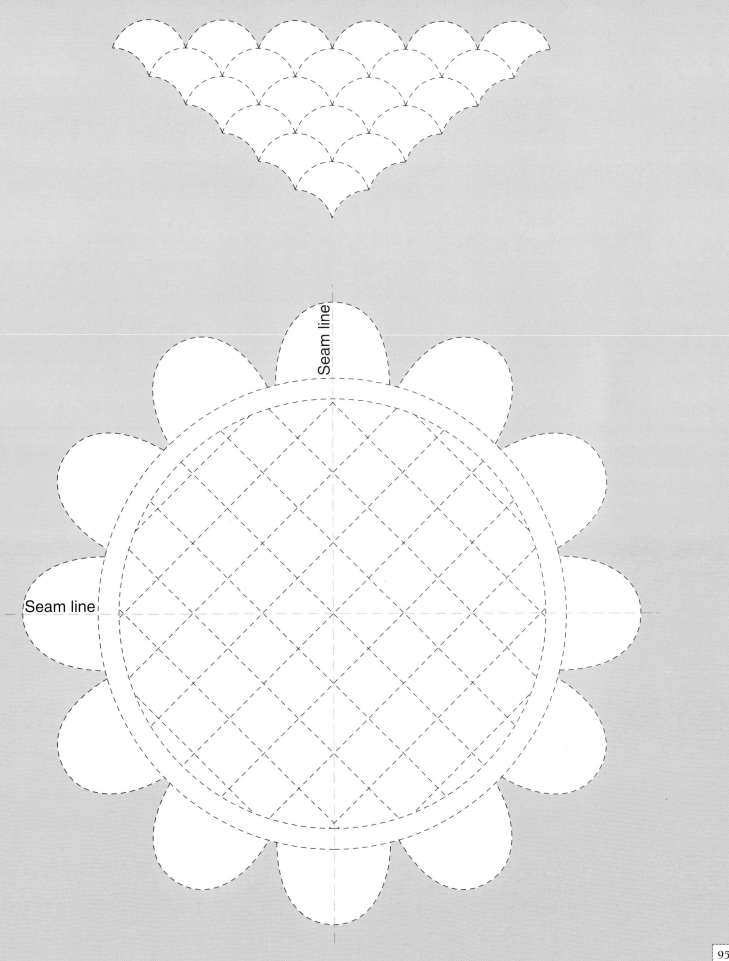

Seam line

Seam line

Join here

Join here

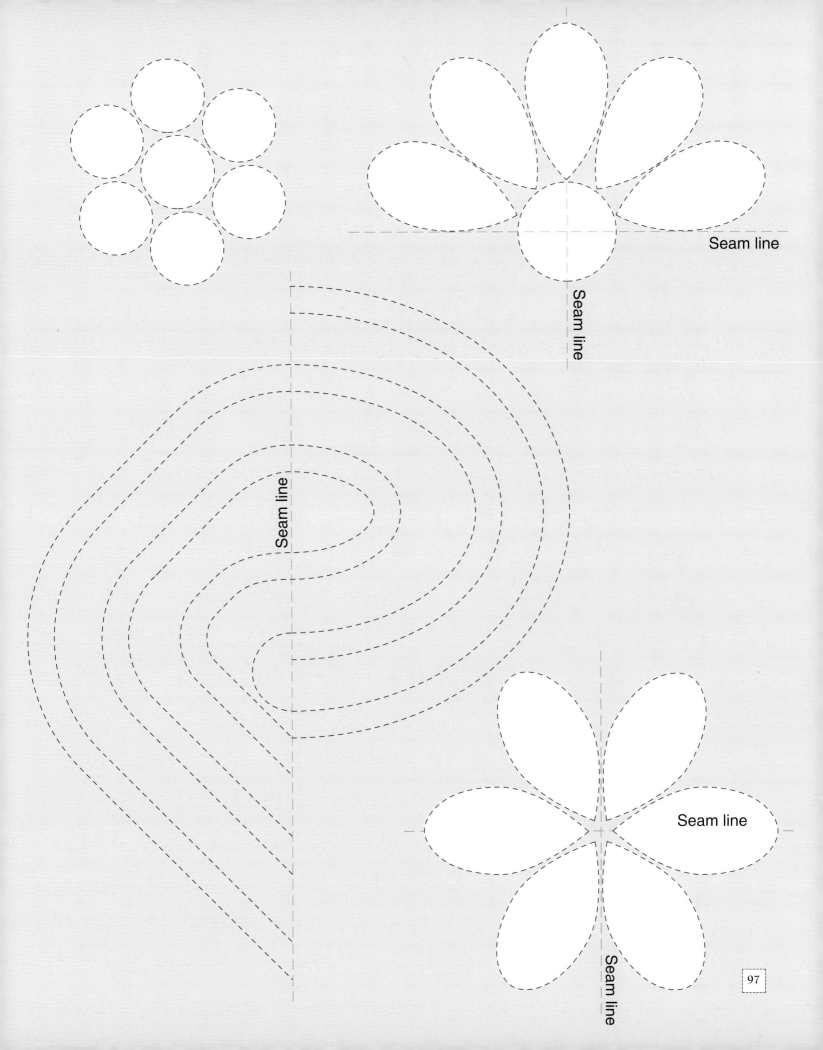

Seam line

Seam line

Seam line

Seam line

Seam line

97

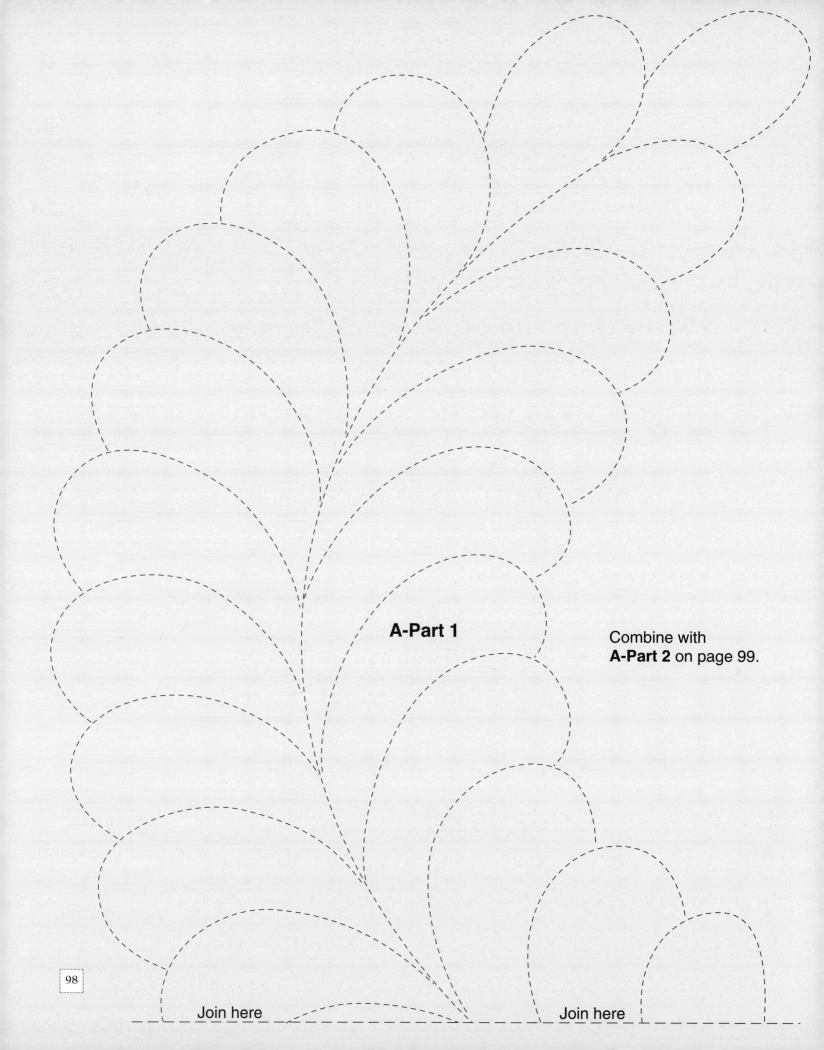

A-Part 1

Combine with
A-Part 2 on page 99.

Join here

Join here

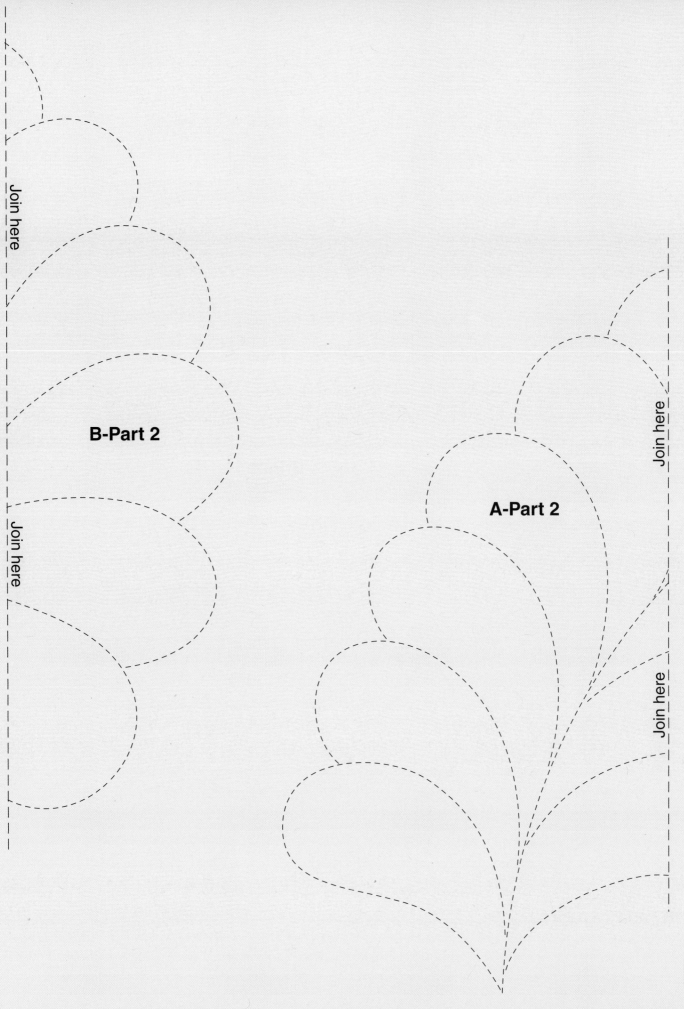

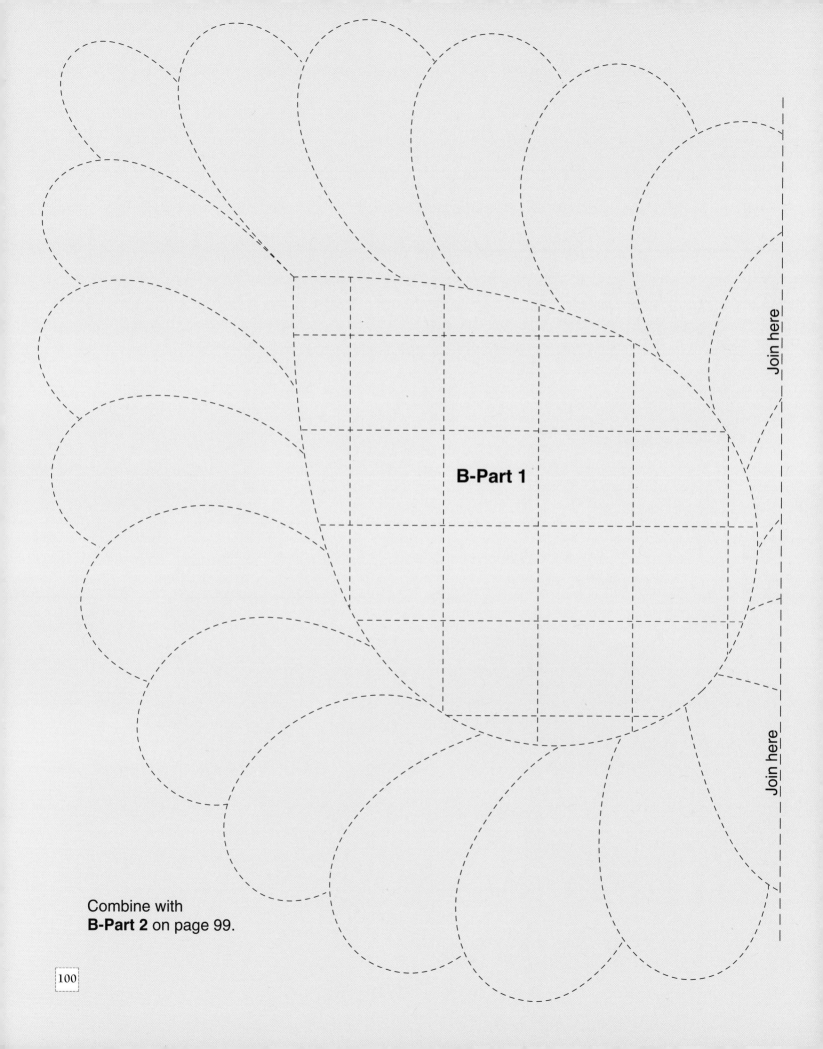

B-Part 1

Combine with
B-Part 2 on page 99.

Design Sources

When we think about where the women who first made red and green appliqué quilts might have gotten ideas and inspiration for their patterns, we can't help noticing strong similarities between designs on the quilts and decoration on practical, everyday objects in the early nineteenth century folk culture. In regions where the quilts first appeared, migrating groups from Europe provided images for painted furniture, *Frakturschriften* (birth and baptismal certificates), embroidered linens, woven coverlets, dishes, and painted tin ware. Designs were passed from one craft form to another. Among the features that stand out in these shared designs are their symmetry and use of geometry to create floral forms.

In the appliqué quilt, symmetrical flower arrangements are dominant, often as vase and flowers designs. A center stem, topped with a large blossom, provides the focus. Two stems with smaller blossoms, exactly alike, are on opposite sides of the center stem. Comparable are the symmetrical flower-filled urns painted on furniture, as, for example, on an 1804 Pennsylvania dower chest, photo 1.

photo 2: Detail of Evans family quilt by Evans family members

Photo 1: Pennsylvania German Chest by John Seltzer, 1804 [Rendering by Frances Lichten]. Image © Board of Trustees, National Gallery of Art, Washington.

The Evans women were among the quilt makers who used the vase and flowers design in an appliqué pattern, photo 2. The quilt pattern is strikingly similar to the design on the dower chest, (pg. 75).

Certain designs can be explained as variations of the vase and flowers. In some, the vase disappears and is replaced by another ornamental device. In the painted decoration on the candle box in photo 3, three tulips sprout from a circular base, and on Rebecca Wilhelm's quilt in photo 4 , flowers spring from a triangular shape.

photo 3: Candle Box [Rendering by Carl Strehlan]. Image © Board of Trustees, National Gallery of Art, Washington.

Photo 4: Detail of Pennsylvania Tulips quilt by Rebecca Wilhelm.

The place of the vase can also be taken by a flower, changing the "sprouting vase" into a "sprouting flower" design in which one flower appears to grow from another, step by step sprouting new leaves or flowers (photo 5).

In yet another variation, the vase is replaced by a "sprouting heart," a motif seen frequently in folk crafts (photo 6). Susan Howerton adapted the sprouting heart design for her quilt (photo 7).

The rosette is another basic form used in appliqué patterns as well as in Germanic decorative folk arts. Historically, two methods

Photo 6: Pennsylvania German Plate, 1824 [Rendering by Aaron Fastovsky] Image © Board of Trustees, National Gallery of Art, Washington.

Photo 7: Detail of Sprouting Hearts quilt by Susan Howerton.

were used to achieve this geometric design. The first was drawn with a straight edge, forming four lines that intersected vertically, horizontally, and diagonally, producing eight sections that could form an eight-pointed star. By rounding the outer edges, an eight-lobed flower-like design resulted. Objects like the 1840 Pennsylvania birth certificate in photo 8 might have inspired women to make rosettes the stylized flowers in their appliqué patterns. Sarah Jane Denny used a rosette in her sprouting flower arrangement, and Sarah Pollock appliquéd six layers of rosettes to make the central motif in her quilt (photo 9).

Although the rosette originated through geometric planning and the use of tools, undoubtedly quiltmakers, familiar with the rosette in other craft forms, could design a simple version

Photo 5: Detail of Rose Tree quilt by Sarah Denny.

Photo 8: Pennsylvania German Birth Certificate, 1840 [Rendering by Albert Levone]. Image © Board of Trustees, National Gallery of Art, Washington.

Photo 9: Detail of Rose and Thistles quilt by Sarah Pollock.

Photo 10: Detail of Rose Appliqué quilt by Isabel Wilson.

by using techniques of paper folding and cutting. Stems and leaves could be added to these more modest rosettes to become blossoms in appliqué patterns (photo 10).

The ten quilts in this book reveal some important aspects in the evolution of a style. Distinctive elements of design were introduced into the red and green appliqué quilts by makers whose sensibilities were shaped by their physical and cultural environments. Appliqué quilt patterns developed with the passage of time and the geographic spread of the red and green type; individual interpretations of recurring designs gave rise to a wide range of pattern variation. But the initial creative choices in the earliest of these designs continued to be reflected in 19th century red and green appliqué quilts—choices that became traditions in our American quilt making heritage.

Garrett, Elisabeth Donaghy. *At Home: The American Family 1750-1870*. New York: Harry N. Abrams, 1990.

Glassie, Henry. *The Spirit of Folk Art*. New York: Harry N. Abrams, 1980.

Lichten, Frances. *Folk Art Motifs of Pennsylvania*. New York: Dover Publications, Inc., 1976.

_____, *Fraktur: The Illuminated Manuscripts of the Pennsylvania Dutch*. Philadelphia: Free Library of Philadelphia, 1958.

Peesch, Reinhard. *The Ornament in European Folk Art*. Transl. Ruth Michaelis-Jenn and Patrick Murray. New York: Alpine Fine Arts Collection, 1982.

Other Star Books

My Quilt Stories
Murder on a Starry Night by Sally Goldenbaum

Project Books:
Fan Quilt Memories
Santa's Parade of Nursery Rhymes